'I urge all to read this book and learn from Tom Wilson's and Riaz Ravat's exciting work in Leicester. This excellent book will develop your understanding of living and integrating in a multicultural society that the UK so clearly is today.'

— *Colonel Stuart Williams, 7th Infantry Brigade, The Desert Rats*

'Modern Britain is diverse and this is an exemplar of imaginative interfaith work from Leicester. Now with much experience of changing contexts, the authors maturely celebrate what is possible whilst addressing the hard challenges. Here we see some next steps to try out as we attempt living well together.'

— *The Very Revd David Monteith, Dean of Leicester*

'Even before moving to Leicester, I had heard much talk of the "Leicester model" of social cohesion. As this book makes clear, there is much that is unique about Leicester, but also much that this wonderful city can teach us about one of the defining questions of our time: how we can learn to live well together.'

— *The Rt Revd Martyn Snow, Bishop of Leicester*

'Undoubtedly a well-researched, highly readable book. It highlights the importance of living well and working together for the shared common good through mutual understanding of the traditions, teachings and practices of diverse communities. The book presents the St Philip's Centre's positive approach to community cohesion and interfaith issues.'

— *Councillor Manjula Sood, Chair, Leicester Council of Faiths*

LEARNING
TO LIVE WELL
TOGETHER

of related interest

Towards Better Disagreement
Religion and Atheism in Dialogue
Paul Hedges
ISBN 978 1 78592 057 8
eISBN 978 1 78450 316 1

Muslim Identity in a Turbulent Age
Islamic Extremism and Western Islamophobia
Edited by Mike Hardy, Fiyaz Mughal and Sarah Markiewicz
Foreword by H.E. Mr Nassir Abdulaziz Al-Nasser
ISBN 978 1 78592 152 0
eISBN 978 1 78450 419 9

Cultural Perspectives on Mental Wellbeing
Spiritual Interpretations of Symptoms in Medical Practice
Natalie Tobert
Foreword by Michael Cornwall
ISBN 978 1 78592 084 4
eISBN 978 1 78450 345 1

The Forgiveness Project
Stories for a Vengeful Age
Marina Cantacuzino
Forewords by Archbishop Emeritus Desmond Tutu and Alexander McCall Smith
ISBN 978 1 84905 566 6 (hardback)
ISBN 978 1 78592 000 4 (paperback)
eISBN 978 1 78450 006 1

LEARNING TO LIVE WELL TOGETHER

CASE STUDIES IN INTERFAITH DIVERSITY

Tom Wilson and Riaz Ravat

Jessica Kingsley *Publishers*
London and Philadelphia

First published in 2017
by Jessica Kingsley Publishers
73 Collier Street
London N1 9BE, UK
and
400 Market Street, Suite 400
Philadelphia, PA 19106, USA

www.jkp.com

Copyright © Tom Wilson and Riaz Ravat 2017

Library of Congress Cataloging in Publication Data
Names: Wilson, Tom, 1943- author.
Title: Learning to live well together : case studies in interfaith diversity
/ Tom Wilson and Riaz Ravat.
Description: Philadelphia : Jessica Kingsley Publishers, 2017. | Includes
bibliographical references and index.
Identifiers: LCCN 2016059646 | ISBN 9781785921940 (alk. paper)
Subjects: LCSH: Religions--Relations--Case studies. | Religious
tolerance--Case studies. | Cultural pluralism--Case studies.
Classification: LCC BL410 .W555 2017 | DDC 201/.5--dc23 LC record
available at https://lccn.loc.gov/2016059646

British Library Cataloguing in Publication Data
A CIP catalogue record for this book is available from the British Library

ISBN 978 1 78592 194 0
eISBN 978 1 78450 467 0

Printed and bound in Great Britain

CONTENTS

Acknowledgements   9

Introduction   11

1. The Leicester Context.   15
   Tom Wilson and Riaz Ravat

2. The St Philip's Centre.   27
   Tom Wilson and Riaz Ravat

3. Encounter.   49
   Tom Wilson

4. Understand.   79
   Tom Wilson

5. Trust   103
   Tom Wilson

6. Co-operate   125
   Tom Wilson

7. Interfaith in the Twenty-first Century.   139
   Riaz Ravat

8. Where Next?   149
   Tom Wilson

References   159

Subject Index   169

Author Index.   175

ACKNOWLEDGEMENTS

We would like to express our grateful thanks to Maureen Hebblewhite, Laura Johnson and John McCallum, colleagues at the St Philip's Centre, who have assisted us in the production of this book. We also are extremely grateful to the different people of faith and no faith with whom we discussed some of the ideas present in this book. We agreed that you would remain anonymous, so we will not name you here. But you know who you are, and we are very thankful for your advice, insight and support. Finally, to you, and all the people of faith, and no faith, that help the St Philip's Centre in its work, we acknowledge a debt that we can never fully repay.

INTRODUCTION

The main aim of the St Philip's Centre is of learning to live well together. We are an accredited provider of learning outside the classroom, and as such our focus is not so much on academic or theoretical study but rather on the learning that comes through meeting different people and exchanging views. Some of our work is rigorously academic and some of the training courses we provide are accredited, but by no means is all of our work conducted in this fashion. The book introduces the St Philip's Centre approach to multifaith engagement and education, using the Centre's strategic aims as an overall framework. Since our focus is primarily on religion as people live it out, there are relatively few academic references in the text, but a great deal of discussion of work with different groups of people.

The issues that the St Philip's Centre tackles are ones which many people are interested in. Community cohesion is often in the headlines, sometimes for positive reasons, such as the accounts of groups of Muslims travelling to Cumbria to help in efforts to clean up after floods. But almost invariably the reasons are more negative. As we were putting the finishing touches to our manuscript, the Casey Review was released (Casey 2016). The recommendations which grabbed headlines concerned the social isolation of Pakistani and Bangladeshi Muslim communities in particular, epitomised by the comment that in one school pupils thought the population of the UK was between 50 and 90 per cent Asian, as such had been their own personal life experience to date. The report made 12 recommendations, including for an increase in investment in teaching English as a second or other language, working to overcome cultural barriers to employment, and introducing stronger safeguards to protect children in unregistered and out-of-hours school settings. In many ways, the report built on the much earlier work by Ted Cantle (Cantle 2001). The question we found ourselves asking is, in 15 years' time, 2031, will another report into integration be produced, and how will it differ from the 2001 and 2016 offerings?

Integration is a loaded word, with implications about imbalance of power, forcing change on one community and apportioning blame. At the St Philip's Centre, we use different language. We talk about learning to live well together, about developing trust and fostering co-operation. Much of our work is in the areas that both Cantle's and Casey's reports covered. However, since our approach is more grassroots based, bottom-up as opposed to top-down, it is well received by the communities we work with.

Chapter 1 introduces the context of Leicester and discusses the so-called 'Leicester model' of social integration. Chapter 2 engages with the overarching theme of living well together. It introduces the St Philip's Centre as an example of an agency working with people of all faiths and no faith. There then follow two case studies, one on a series of conferences that the Centre has conducted in partnership with the Church of England's National Education Office, on the theme of 'Living Well Together'. The second gives an example of our training offer for public sector organisations.

Chapter 3 discusses encounter, explaining how to facilitate good encounters between people of different faiths or no faith. The two case studies in this chapter are of work with the armed forces and with medical students. Chapter 4 takes understanding of different religious perspectives as the main theme. The focus is on brief overviews of the diversity within the Jewish, Christian, Muslim, Hindu, Buddhist and Sikh religions. Chapter 5 focuses on the development of trust. The chapter begins by explaining why the Centre uses trust, and not tolerance, respect or honour, as a key criterion for evaluating our work. The discussion moves on to how trust can be developed and includes a more in-depth look at one key area of the Centre's work, namely the Prevent strategy. Chapter 6 gives examples of co-operation. There are brief discussions of two areas where the Centre has done a small amount of work, namely in responding to child sexual exploitation and hate crime. The bulk of the chapter examines the Near Neighbours programme, and includes several case studies of projects supported by the work. Chapter 7 examines twenty-first-century interfaith work, using the example of the Catalyst programme.

Chapter 8 asks, 'Where next?' The chapter proposes a three-stage model for learning to live well together in the future. First, we must acknowledge what is, making a realistic assessment of the current situation that we face. Second, we imagine what could be, taking in a wide variety of views and perspectives. Third, we decide together how we can get there.

The book is a joint project between ourselves, the director (Tom) and deputy director (Riaz) of the St Philip's Centre. We have indicated at the start of each chapter whether one or both of us have been involved in writing it. We are grateful for the support, encouragement and advice of many colleagues and friends without whose help this book could not have been written.

1

THE LEICESTER CONTEXT

TOM WILSON AND RIAZ RAVAT

> Our community has been too isolated. Before I went
> on the Catalyst programme, I did not have any friends
> who were not Jewish. Having taken part, we have
> resolved to set up an interfaith group in our school, to
> make sure more of our friends get to meet with people
> of other faiths. We have been too inward looking. We
> need to change.

Those were not his exact words, but they were the
sentiments expressed. The young man, who is himself a
committed Jew, was speaking at the annual Lambeth Palace
interfaith reception in May 2016. He is a graduate of the
Catalyst Young Leaders Programme, of which more in
Chapter 7. The St Philip's Centre runs Catalyst on behalf
of the Near Neighbours programme (the Bradford-based
Faithful Neighbourhood Centre delivers in other areas of
the country). He had attended the West London Catalyst
course in 2015 and was reflecting on his experience to a
very distinguished audience, including both the chief
rabbi and the president of the Board of Deputies of
British Jews. Sometimes young people will say what their
elders fear. Sometimes people within a community are the
best placed to challenge an insular, isolating world view.

The courage to speak honestly in this way is a necessary precursor to learning to live well together.

The thesis of this book is that we must learn to live well together if we are to develop a positive society, where difference and conflict are seen as opportunities for growth, and diversity is celebrated and not feared. This first main chapter explains the lessons that Leicester has to offer the rest of the world in how to go about this, and subsequent chapters put flesh on the bones that are outlined here.

We begin with the phrase 'learning to live well together'. The intention expressed by 'learning' is important. Living well together does not just happen. It is a complex adaptive problem, which requires creative thinking, courageous action and the humility to recognise and move on from mistakes. No simple technical solutions will work. Social engineering, where people of different ethnicities are forced to live next to each other, or made to encounter each other in overly formalised sterile settings, does not lead to real learning. At best, participants offer a begrudging lip service which has little lived reality. Forced integration rarely results in real integration but only parallel lives.

Rather, we must decide we want to learn about the other. We need a disposition for encounter, for relishing difference, for seeing the other as someone who can teach us, enable us to flourish and develop a clearer understanding of our own identity. This process is messy, highly emotionally charged, very complicated but also enormous fun. Throughout this book, we are inviting you to come on a learning journey with us, as we explain our learning and experience in living well together.

The chapter begins with an introduction to the city of Leicester before introducing and explaining the 'Leicester model'.

Introduction to the city of Leicester

The most diverse city on the planet

In 2013 the *Independent* newspaper described Leicester as 'the most multicultural city on the planet'. In December 2015 a study by Suzanne Hall, Julia King and Robin Finlay from the London School of Economics suggested that Narborough Road, one of the main routes into the city, is the most diverse street in Europe, with 22 ethnicities and communities represented. It has not always been this way. Those who live in Leicester have had to learn how to live well together, and this has not always been an easy process.

Early history and populations

Two thousand or so years ago the Romans named the city *Ratae Coritanum*. The Saxons subsequently conquered it, and the city was also part of the Danish conquests known as the Danegeld. In the eleventh century it became Norman territory. The population was small, about 3000 families, until the eighteenth century when people flooded in from the countryside, taking Leicester to 150,000 in 1760. Victorian Leicester grew further, and the present population is around 300,000, with another 600,000 in the County of Leicestershire.

Twentieth-century migration and the present day

Victorian Leicester (1837–1901) already had significant Irish minorities and small numbers of Jewish and German economic migrants from 1890. This led to Leicester becoming one of the richest cities on the continent. In the period after 1940 Leicester experienced an influx of West

Indians who came to fight in the Second World War and then as single male economic migrants. They faced a colour bar and extreme racism. Many left mainline churches, of which they had been members in the Caribbean, to form their own black churches such as the New Testament Church of God. Some are Pentecostal in style; the majority are in the Highfields area.

In the 1960s migrants from India and Pakistan arrived as single men to work in public services. East Europeans from Poland, Serbia, Latvia and Estonia also arrived in thousands. All these migrants lived in Highfields, the old Irish and railway workers' area behind the railway station on London Road. It became known to whites as the 'Khyber Pass'. Following independence in East Africa, Leicester received 60,000 Asians in waves, from Tanzania, Kenya, Uganda, Malawi, Zimbabwe and elsewhere. The largest group were the group Idi Amin expelled from Uganda in 1973. Originally Leicester did not welcome these migrants, with the Labour Council of the time taking out adverts in Kampala newspapers, aimed at deterring new arrivals.

'Present conditions in the city are very different from those met by earlier settlers' read Leicester's advert in the Uganda *Argus*. In particular, it went on, there were 'several thousands of families on the housing list', 'hundreds of children…awaiting places in schools', while social and health services were 'already stretched to the limit' (Popham 2013). The basic message was: 'Leicester is full.' It failed completely as a deterrent; in fact, it had precisely the opposite impact, drawing Leicester to the attention of potential migrants who might otherwise have settled in other English cities. This hesitancy about receiving migrants is often missed in contemporary celebrations of the diversity of the city but must be remembered. Suspicion of migrants is by no means new.

Between 1968 and 1975 the ethnic minority population of the city rose considerably. The newcomers were in family groups, with full citizenship and initially via the Punjab to be followed by people from the Gujarat state of India directly or via Africa – the latter becoming known as 'twice migrants'. They encountered a racist backlash in the form of the National Front (now the British National Party), who gained 25 per cent of the vote in Leicester in 1976 with the slogan 'Stop Immigration! Start repatriation!' Their vote collapsed with the election of Margaret Thatcher in 1979, and they are now only active in pockets of the county. The city itself, with its encouragement and funding of the Leicester Council of Faiths as early as 1986, took proactive steps to counter their influence.

Asian people weathered the abuse and hostility, turning to politics. In 1983 and 1987 large numbers of Asian Labour councillors were elected. In 1987, an Asian Lord Mayor and an Asian MP were selected and elected respectively for the first time. In 2001 many councillors lost their seats to new Indian Muslim Liberal Democrats in response to the Iraq War. Labour lost control to the Liberal Democrats for the first time for 24 years. As well as achieving a political breakthrough, since the 1970s Asian entrepreneurs have rapidly set up corner shops, and then businesses in food, textiles, property and land, just when Leicester's traditional industries (shoes, textiles and light engineering) were in steep decline.

Since this time the ethnic minority population of the city has risen to 28 per cent in 1991, 36 per cent in 2001 and 49.4 per cent in 2011. The 2011 Census revealed a small majority for 'White' and 'White'-related groups but ethnic minority communities already make up over half of the numbers in city schools. At the time of writing, Leicester is the UK's most plural city.

The city is currently drawing in communities from Poland, Slovakia, Iraq and Zimbabwe, the Kurdish region of the Middle East, as well as an estimated 10,000 Somalis, mostly via Holland, Denmark and Sweden. There are several thousand Roma from central Europe as well, who are under the radar. Leicester City Council has managed this process well over the past 30 years, avoiding riots (with the exception of 1981) and turning clients into partners in that time. Leicester is seen as an international model of good race relations. There is a theory that the (twice-migrant) South Asian population of Leicester comprises communities that previously lived fairly harmoniously together before coming to the UK and that they have simply carried on in this vein, whereas in other cities the contemporary population is made up of groups that have a history of antagonism. Whether this is a sufficient explanation is a moot point, but versions of it are aired in discussions of Leicester's relatively peaceful multiculturalism.

As Figure 1.1 shows, according to the 2011 Census, Christianity is now the faith of 32.4 per cent of people in Leicester (44 per cent in 2001). The figure for England and Wales is 59.3 per cent. Leicester has a Non-conformist Dissenter history, so Anglo Catholicism is rather weak here. There are some Asian Christians, many of whom are Catholics with roots in India. Former bishops of Leicester, the Rt Revd Tom Butler and the Rt Revd Tim Stevens, have actively encouraged interfaith dialogue and created expertise in a small cadre of Anglican priests, a tradition continued by the current bishop, the Rt Revd Martyn Snow. The Methodist Church also has a long history in this field in Leicester, and there has been a limited involvement from other churches. St Philip's Centre is at the heart of this Christian work. The Centre was founded by the Revd Canon Dr Andrew Wingate OBE, working with the Rt Revd Richard Atkinson OBE and Kathy Morrison MBE.

Subsequent to Andrew's retirement the director was the Revd Canon Dr John Hall and is now the Revd Dr Tom Wilson, co-author of this book.

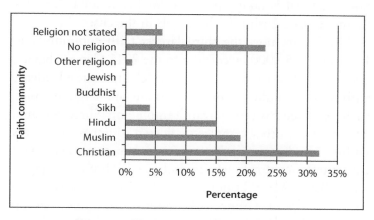

Figure 1.1 The faith communities of Leicester, according to the 2011 Census

The Muslim community is growing rapidly and is now the second largest faith in the city (c. 61,500 people). It is based primarily on five ethnic blocs: Indian Muslims including Indian Africans (the largest), Somalis, Pakistanis, Arabs and Bangladeshis. There are an estimated 60 mosques and over 100 madrassas (supplementary schools). The majority are Sunni places of worship, but there are also Shi'a communities. Leicester houses many faiths but also several traditions within faiths, so the city is home to sub-traditions such as the Ismaili and Dawoodi Bohra communities – both widely regarded as part of the wider Shi'a Muslim fabric. There is an umbrella group called the Federation of Muslim Organisations (FMO), which has been in existence for over 30 years, and a Muslim Burial Council of Leicestershire. It is difficult to be certain about the exact number of Muslims in the city, as it is suggested that not everyone completes the religious affiliation on census forms; similarly, there is no compulsory registration of either mosques or madrassas, so a terraced house could become a 'house mosque' or a front room could be used daily as a madrassa with hardly anyone noticing what is taking place. As well as many madrassas, there are also Muslim faith schools in the city.

Hindus are now the third largest faith community in Leicester (c. 50,000) according to the 2011 Census, having historically been second, a fact which has caused unease within the Hindu community. There are large temples, such as Shree Swaminarayan Temple and Shree Sanatan Mandir, with other temples dedicated to gurus or strands within Hinduism. Each caste and sub-caste also have community centres such as Lohana-Brahmin, Prajapati and Mistry. Most Hindus in Leicester are Gujarati by background, with a minority from Punjab and an increasing number of Sri Lankan Tamils and South Indians. Visits by gurus attract many thousands, and Diwali and Navratri are very popular festivals in Leicester, even amongst non-Hindus, and receive national coverage (Sillitoe 2015). The city council estimates that 35,000 attended the Diwali light switch on in 2016 (Visit Leicester 2016). Gujarati Hindus are prosperous, with middle classes moving into wealthier areas such as Oadby and Syston. They are a highly educated community with strong vested interests in India. At a corporate level Leicester is twinned with Rajkot in the Indian state of Gujarat. There is a Krishna Avanti Primary School in Leicester, and permission has recently been granted by the Department for Education for another primary school and a secondary school to be built by the same trust.

The Sikh community has a significant presence in the city and the county; indeed it is the largest Sikh community in the East Midlands. Many of the Sikh community migrated directly from India in the 1950s and were in Leicester long before the so-called 'twice migrants' arrived from East Africa. Vaisakhi is a major festival in Leicester. The April 2016 parade involved 15,000 participants (Frodsham 2016). There are Sikh museums at the Guru Nanak and Guru Tegh Bahadur gurdwaras. The Sikh community has a particular interest in the involvement of Sikhs in the British armed forces and makes a point of celebrating their history, of both co-operation and conflict, as the recently launched Sikh Museum Initiative on the Anglo-Sikh wars of 1845–9 makes clear (Anglo-Sikh Wars 2016). Sikhs often hold major collection drives for food and clothing during Vaisakhi. Gurdwaras provide free meals to members of all communities. This community meal is called *langar*. Each year Hindu, Sikh, Buddhist and Jain communities work with the St Philip's Centre for a Sewa Day social action charitable project (of which more in Chapter 7). As well as serving community meals, gurdwaras in Leicester also provide community facilities, such as a gym, adult day care centre, pre-school and Punjabi classes. There is a recently established Sikh primary school in Leicester, Falcons School, which celebrated its second birthday in the academic year 2016/17, and began taking in pupils from Reception to Year 4.

There are smaller faiths with hundreds of members in the county too. Jainism has a beautiful temple in Oxford Street in the city, the first Jain temple built in Western Europe. Judaism has two synagogues; one progressive and one orthodox. They both come together each year for the Mitzvah Day social action charitable effort which the St Philip's Centre is involved in. Baha'is have a small but active presence and there are five Buddhist temples in the county. There is also an active Pagan community, although since Paganism is a very individualistic pursuit it is difficult to ascertain numbers.

It should be noted that faiths do not follow local authority borders. There have always been significant numbers of faiths other than Christian in the university town of Loughborough. The Loughborough Council of Faiths has membership from the Baha'i, Brahma Kumaris, Christian, Hindu, Mormon, Muslim, Pagan, Quaker and Sikh communities. Moreover, recent years have also begun to show a significant move outwards from Leicester of more affluent members of the Asian communities. This has meant that Oadby, just outside the city boundary, has become very multifaith, with places of worship being established. Other areas of the county such as Hinckley, Birstall, Syston, Thurmaston, Great Glen, Glenfield and Market Harborough have smaller numbers at the moment but these numbers are increasing.

There are a number of mechanisms enabling different communities to meet in order to discuss matters of common concern. These include the Faith Leaders Forum, which is chaired by the Bishop of Leicester, the Leicester City Mayor's Faith and Community Forum, the Leicester Council of Faiths, Loughborough Council of Faiths and the Leicestershire Interfaith Forum.

The 'Leicester model'

Those who work in integration and community cohesion do sometimes mention the concept of the 'Leicester model' of social integration. The 'Leicester model' is normally taken as a sign of positive social cohesion. Take the spike in reported hate crime in the immediate run up to and aftermath of the EU referendum in June 2016. Nationally, a five-fold increase was reported, but in Leicester the BBC reported the figure was only double (BBC 2016a). Even a doubling of hate crime is unacceptable, but what caused the increase to be less than the national picture?

How has Leicester avoided the problems that some other communities have faced?

There is no simple formula, but a number of factors are relevant. First, there is the size of Leicester. It is a well-networked and compact city which is relatively quick and straightforward to get around. This means it is easy for people to meet each other, and the same people see each other regularly and in a variety of contexts. Those involved in the civic life of the city are able to establish long-term relationships of trust and co-operation. Different-sized communities require different models of integration and engagement. What works well in Leicester will not necessarily work in London or Loughborough, as the former is much bigger and the latter smaller. Second, there is the fact that no one community is truly dominant. Less than 50 per cent of the population of the city is of Caucasian heritage (although that is only a recent development). Equally, the Hindu and Muslim populations are a similar proportion of the overall population of the city. Third, there is significant diversity within the communities. There is no single monolithic Hindu or Muslim or Christian bloc who dominate interfaith engagement. Fourth, many of the 'twice migrants' had already lived alongside each other in East Africa before they moved to Leicester. Muslims, Hindus and Sikhs, all of whom had moved from the Indian sub-continent to East Africa in search of work, were in the habit of celebrating each other's festivals and had similar cultural outlooks. So a Muslim whose family origins were in Gujarat may in fact share more culturally with a Christian or Hindu with the same background than with a fellow Muslim whose family origins lie in Pakistan or Somalia. Fifth, many of those who moved to Leicester had previous experience of running businesses or working in professional trades. They were therefore better able to find good employment quickly and were also better placed to navigate the collapse of the traditional textile industries than those in other cities in the UK. Sixth, the fact of continual migration from a wide range of countries means the city council are continually learning how to welcome new arrivals.

Although these different factors have been listed, they are not in order of priority. Rather they combine together to provide a welcoming set of conditions which enable people to learn how to live well together. That is not to say that everything is positive. Leicester certainly faces many challenges. As with many cities where there is diversity, there is a tendency for people of particular ethnic or cultural backgrounds to cluster together. There has been a degree of 'white flight', whereby Caucasian families have moved out of the inner city to the surrounding market towns and villages of Leicestershire. More recently, there has also been 'Asian flight', whereby the more affluent of Asian heritage have also moved out of the centre of Leicester into the suburbs and to the market towns and villages. Many return to the city centre to participate in religious activities but their homes are now elsewhere.

2

THE ST PHILIP'S CENTRE

TOM WILSON AND RIAZ RAVAT

The St Philip's Centre is an ecumenical Christian charity publicly incorporated on 2 June 2006 by representatives of the Anglican Diocese of Leicester; the Parochial Church Council of St Philip's Church; the East Midlands Synod of the United Reformed Church; the Oxford and Leicester District of the Methodist Church (now the Northampton District); and the Roman Catholic Diocese of Nottingham, with the following aims:

1. Equipping Christians and others to live and work in a multifaith society.

2. Providing opportunities to reflect on Christian mission, presence, engagement, dialogue and evangelism in a multifaith world.

3. Offering consultancy and training services to enable people and communities in Leicester and beyond to live together in harmony.

4. Sharing regionally, nationally and internationally the experience and expertise gained from the objectives in 1, 2 and 3 above.

The St Philip's Centre is a resourcing, not a representative, organisation. We do not work in isolation but in relationship with a wide variety of groups and professional bodies. Our partnerships are always established for a purpose, to meet shared objectives, mutually enhance delivery of services and further the common good. We have three main areas of focus. First, the delivery of experience-based education and training. Second, resourcing and equipping those at the grassroots. Third, developing and supporting those within positions of influence at all levels, especially but not exclusively within the Church and other faith communities.

The education and training work engages a wide variety of people, from primary school children to old age pensioners, as well as professionals involved with the armed forces, healthcare, the police, offender management and managers in private companies. Work for the common good includes organising vigils and other responses to times of national tension or tragedy, as well as resourcing efforts to tackle complex issues such as child sexual exploitation or hate crime. Work with churches focuses on equipping them to better understand the complex multifaith world in which they operate. Other major areas of work relate to Prevent and Near Neighbours, both central government initiatives which are explained in further detail in subsequent chapters.

Theological foundations

The St Philip's Centre works for the public good, and does so from a Christian foundation. The Centre's current strategic plan states:

> We aim to fulfil what Jesus says are the two great commandments to love God and our neighbours as ourselves. The church describes God as Trinity and Christians believe God to be relational. This belief in

the importance of relationship inspires us to work hard at articulating and engaging with diverse Christian understandings of this inheritance of faith. Moreover, part of the foundational understanding of the St Philip's Centre as a Christian organisation is therefore that we are to relate to others, both those who are similar to us and also those who are very different. The St Philip's Centre is founded on the understanding that every human being is unique, all of us are intrinsically valuable and all of us need help to become the individuals we were created to be. The St Philip's Centre recognises the complexity of the world, the church, and other faith communities and that we are called to take risks and to actively engage with the other.

The St Philip's Centre accepts that all those involved with the Centre do not necessarily believe in the same way. We embrace people from a wide variety of perspectives and backgrounds to serve the common good, which we understand to be founded upon the ethos and values derived from the Christian foundation of the Centre.

The Centre is thus rooted in the Christian tradition, but in a generous and open way, enabling people of all faiths and no faith to be employed by and work in close partnership with the Centre.

Stakeholders

As well as the original founding partner churches, the St Philip's Centre has established good working relationships with many other Christian groups. These include but are not limited to the Anglican Diocese of Southwell and Nottingham, the Anglican Diocese of Peterborough and the Baptist Union of Great Britain. The Centre also enjoys good working relationships with local public sector organisations, especially Leicester City Council, Leicestershire County Council and Leicestershire Police, as well as with local army regiments, especially the Seventh Brigade and 158 Regiment RLC. The Centre has significant partnerships with a wide range of educational institutions, including De Montfort University, the University of Leicester, Loughborough University and Leicester College, as well as numerous schools and colleges in Leicester, Leicestershire, Lincolnshire, Northamptonshire, Cambridgeshire and even further afield. Moreover, the Centre enjoys good working relationships with national government departments, notably the Home Office, the Ministry of Defence, the Department for Communities and Local Government, and the Foreign and Commonwealth Office. The Centre has worked closely with the Church Urban Fund in the delivery of the Near Neighbours programme, and with national organisations such as the Board of Deputies of British Jews, the Inter Faith Network for the UK and the Christian–Muslim Forum.

All of the Centre's work relies on the goodwill and co-operation of all of these stakeholders. Crucially our future success depends on developing and maintaining strong relationships with local people of faith. The St Philip's Centre is very grateful for the support offered to our work by so many individuals and organisations, especially within the City of Leicester. These are far too numerous to mention here, but are nevertheless recognised and respected as key stakeholders in the work of the Centre.

The Centre's values

Figure 2.1 illustrates the Centre's values. The current vision of the St Philip's Centre is of 'Learning to Live Together'. The notion of learning is an active one, but one based in grassroots, community settings, rather than in the isolation of academia or the public policy sector. The whole phrase can be taken as an invitation to actively learning about how an individual or specific community should live appropriately in modern society whilst also emphasising that this learning cannot be done in isolation; we learn how to live with others by being with others. The phrase is expanded for the title of this book, emphasising the idea of learning how to achieve the best possible coexistence, but it is deliberately compact when used as a strap line for the Centre.

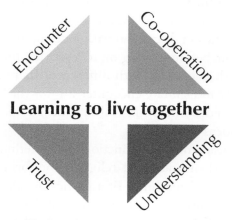

Figure 2.1 The St Philip's Centre's current vision and values

There are four values used to give concrete shape to this vision. These are: *encounter, understand, trust* and *co-operate*. We will first examine the possible linear developmental progression they have before expanding on how else they interact with each other. Detailed exploration of these values forms the bulk of this book.

A lot of the work that the St Philip's Centre does is simply enabling people to encounter difference. There is a natural human tendency for us to seek out people who are like ourselves. But if we surround ourselves with similarity, we lose the capacity to live well with those who are different; moreover, a failure to encounter the other can mean we develop fears of them. These seeds of fear may take root in our subconscious and grow into plants of prejudice and even hatred. Furthermore, being surrounded by similarity can stunt our own growth and development into rounded human beings. If these problems are to be overcome, we must encounter difference.

These encounters may mean meeting and conversing with people from another faith community. It may be a simple practical exercise, such as a visit to a place of worship of another faith. One tool is something we call 'speed faithing', or a 'round robin', where groups of visitors spend 15 or 20 minutes in discussion with a person of a different faith tradition, before moving on to a second, third, fourth and even fifth encounter with difference. There are many different ways to facilitate encounter, but for the St Philip's Centre such encounters must always be between people, not simply ideas or theories.

Within academia a distinction is sometimes drawn between 'doctrinal' and 'lived' religion. The former are the theoretical, formal teachings of a particular faith, and the latter relates to how people actually live out that faith in day-to-day reality. Thus, for example, within Christianity there is an important doctrinal teaching of Jesus that Christians should 'love your enemies and pray for those who persecute you' (Matthew 5.43–48), and similarly the Apostle Paul instructs Christians to not take revenge (Romans 12.19). But the reality is that Christians do often hate others, plot revenge against them and so forth. A second example might be the prohibition within Islam against the consumption of alcohol. Whilst that is a clear doctrinal teaching, the lived faith of at least some who would self-identify as Muslims does include the consumption of alcohol, especially in the privacy of their own homes.

Such differences raise questions. Take the Jewish *kashrut* (religious dietary) laws as an example. There is a wide range of understanding within modern Judaism as to how to observe *kashrut* within daily life. For a non-Jew to understand the breadth of modern Judaism, encounter with a variety of Jews is crucial, as it is only through face-to-face engagement that it is possible to develop an understanding of how different people understand, interpret and live out a particular faith tradition.

The basic principles are fairly straightforward to explain:

1. Certain animals may not be eaten at all. This restriction includes the flesh, organs, eggs and milk of the forbidden animals.

2. Of the animals that may be eaten, the birds and mammals must be killed in accordance with Jewish law.

3. All blood must be drained from the meat or broiled out of it before it is eaten.

4. Certain parts of permitted animals may not be eaten.

5. Meat (the flesh of birds and mammals) cannot be eaten with dairy. Fish, eggs, fruits, vegetables and grains can be eaten with either meat or dairy. (According to some views, fish may not be eaten with meat.)

6. Utensils that have come into contact with meat may not be used with dairy, and vice versa. Utensils that have come into contact with non-kosher food may not be used with kosher food. This applies only where the contact occurred while the food was hot.

7. Grape products made by non-Jews may not be eaten.

(Bard 1998)

For those Jews who wish to follow these rules, it is relatively simple to do so at home, after the initial organisation of ensuring there are separate spaces within the kitchen for the preparation of meat and dairy foods. The challenge comes when eating in restaurants or other people's homes. Different Jews form different opinions as to what is the best way of observing the *kashrut* laws, including how restrictive they should be of engagement with public and civic life. For some Jews, the food must be prepared in a suitably certified and inspected kitchen; others are happy to eat any vegetarian food, to give two examples amongst the wide range of possible opinions. It is difficult, on paper, to give a clear account of how a particular individual's choice in how to observe these laws is an expression of their Jewish cultural and religious identity. The only way to really understand these nuances is to have conversations with a number of Jews and understand their range of opinions. A few examples will illustrate the point.

For some Jews, the *kashrut* legislation has little impact on their daily life. It is unlikely to have no impact at all, as even the most non-observant Jews would probably abstain from eating pork products. Moreover, whilst a Jew might not observe the *kashrut* laws in day-to-day living, when it came to celebrating *Pesach* (Passover), they would be likely to clean their kitchen to remove all traces of leaven and avoid eating any products which contained leaven or yeast during the celebrations.

Personal circumstances also impact the type of observance. An Orthodox Jewish understanding of *kashrut* would mean that a kitchen should have two sinks, two sets of cutlery and crockery and so forth, one for meat products and one for milk products. However, this requires a reasonable-sized kitchen, and so moving to a smaller house might mean a conscious decision to stop eating any meat products rather than cross-contaminate by having utensils involved in the preparation of milk and meat products in the same sink. For those who wish to be very strict, and use entirely separate appliances during *Pesach*, this would require owning four dishwashers (one for milk for regular use, one for meat for regular use, one for milk for *Pesach*, and one for meat during *Pesach*). Being able to afford four dishwashers (and have the two kitchens, one for meat and one for milk) to accommodate them is not something most people could afford, and hence some sort of a compromise must be made. Certified kosher meat is more expensive than regular meat, because the cost includes paying the wages of those who inspect the slaughter process. Thus, pragmatic factors such as income levels can have a significant impact on the nature of observance of these laws.

The degree of religious observance is also crucial. Take cheese as an example. Rennet, crucial in cheese production, is often taken from the stomach of recently slaughtered newly born baby cows. If rennet is used in cheese production, then the cheese would no longer be kosher, and a strict Orthodox Jew would therefore not eat it. Some Jews would argue that the amount of rennet present in the cheese they eat in a sandwich is so small, it does not matter. They follow a ruling that if the proportion of non-kosher food present is smaller than an olive, then it does not contaminate the meal. Still others would think the whole debate was unnecessarily pedantic and against the spirit of the ruling entirely. It is important to remember that those who follow *kashrut* laws are not doing so because they are pedantic or awkward, but because they believe they are following divine commands. Devout Jews follow the dietary requirements of their faith because they believe that in doing so they are living out their calling to be set apart, holy, God's chosen people, whose role is to be a blessing to the whole world. When you encounter difference, then building relationship which enables you to develop a nuanced understanding of motivation and lived faith is more important than memorising the details of lived religious practice.

Once we have encountered difference and begun to understand why people believe what they believe and live as they do, there is a real possibility that we can develop greater trust for each other. As the staff and trustees of the St Philip's Centre debated this third value, we examined three other words, each of which were rejected for specific reasons. The notion of tolerance was rejected fairly quickly, because we understood tolerance to be a very limited virtue. Tolerance, we reflected, has connotations of begrudging acceptance; of allowing existence within clearly defined limits; of not really wanting the other to be there but not having the option of removing them. Some may think this an overly harsh rejection of the term. It is true that some people advocate tolerance from entirely positive motivations. But it remains limited; if we only tolerate the other, how far will we go in learning to live well together?

The second term that was rejected was 'respect'. We recognise that respect is of greater significance than tolerance; that it is a further development of appreciation for the other. But respect does not necessarily imply close engagement with the other. It is possible to respect someone's position without really knowing them as a person; indeed, the idea of respecting another can become a defence against the need to get to know them. The third term, honour, was rejected on similar grounds. One can honour the contribution of another without necessarily relating to them well.

Trust does not necessarily require agreement. Indeed, if we are to learn to live well together with those who are different from ourselves, then whilst it is important that we encounter them and understand them, it is vital that we do not insist we must agree. Attempts to develop lowest common denominator points of agreement do not lead to trust and co-operation, but to bland statements suitable for dissemination as the proceedings of conferences of the professional interfaith circuit. Trust is necessary for a good working relationship. Agreement is not; indeed, constructive disagreement can be the catalyst for dynamic action as we co-operate together.

We can only learn to live well together if we co-operate with each other. No one person or faith community has all of the solutions to the many different challenges we face as a society. Many of the solutions can only be realised if we work together, as the problems are broader than those of any particular faith community. Encounter can develop into understanding, creating the conditions for trust to flourish and enabling co-operation on areas of common concern. The Salaam Shalom Kitchen (SaSh), a joint initiative of Nottingham Liberal Synagogue and not-for-profit Muslim organisation Himmah, is a good example of how these four values might play out in practice. Initially started as an initiative funded by the Near Neighbours small grants programme (of which more in a subsequent chapter), it has been running since May 2015 and has now achieved independent status, although it remains dependent on donations to cover ongoing running costs. Muslims and Jews encountered each other, understood both their differences and their common concern, developed trust for each other and now co-operate in running a weekly drop-in café for the homeless.

The four values of the St Philip's Centre do not necessarily interact in a solely linear fashion. Co-operation may be the basis for encounter. New volunteers joining projects such as the SaSh kitchen, for example, begin by co-operating with each other, and through volunteering together encounter difference and develop understanding of each other. A desire to understand difference may be the motivation behind a search for encounter. And so on.

This book is organised in the linear fashion followed above, but each chapter notes different stages at which that particular value can become important. A final point to note is that encounter with difference may happen as much within a particular faith community as between faith communities. Indeed, intrafaith encounter may be far more complex and challenging than interfaith encounter. Enabling Hindus to trust and co-operate with those Hindus within the ISKCON (International Society for Krishna Consciousness, or Hare Krishna) movement can be a challenge. It can be hard to enable trust and co-operation even within a particular grouping or denomination, as various public debates within the worldwide Anglican Communion make clear. People of a particular disposition may find they have more in common with those of other faith traditions who share their disposition, than with those of their own faith. Thus, for example, ultra-Orthodox Jews and Muslims are united in concern to protect their rights to raising their children in solely Jewish or Muslim environments. Equally, those actively campaigning for the rights of lesbian, gay, bisexual and transgender (LGBT) people of faith may form alliances across different faiths rather than with those who have different views but share the same faith tradition. This is a complex world where answers are not straightforward, but the opportunities for learning and growth are immense.

The chapter closes with two case studies of work the St Philip's Centre has been involved with around the general theme of learning to live well together. They are included to illustrate the points made in the chapter and to provide material for reflection and discussion.

CASE STUDY 2.1: ANGLICAN EDUCATION

TOM WILSON

The education sector is one important area that should facilitate learning to live well together. The St Philip's Centre, in partnership with the National Education Office of the Church of England, has been running a series of events on precisely this theme.

On 8 December 2015 a group gathered in Church House, Westminster, to discuss the theme of 'Living Well Together'. The day focused on two key questions. First, how does the education provided and the ethos lived out in our education establishments foster living well together? Second, what challenges do education establishments face in promoting living well together and how can these be overcome?

The initial stimulus for the day was the debate over exactly what constitutes 'British values' and how they should best be taught in schools. Rather than generate an overly negative focus on aspects of educational policy that are contentious, the planning team decided to invite religious participants from a variety of faith backgrounds and educational settings to contribute to a positive discussion on how religious faith both helps and hinders our living well together as a cohesive society. At the outset, we recognised that the place of religion in public society today is contested. Moreover, it is evident that a very small minority of religious people act in a way that divides and hinders our living well together in diversity in modern Britain today. Whilst this is the case, we believe that the vast majority of such contributions are positive and that these positive contributions should be highlighted and showcased. Furthermore, many religious foundation schools have a very positive track record in equipping pupils to live well together. This belief was confirmed when, following his visit to the Living Well

Together day conference, Lord Nash, parliamentary under-secretary of state for schools, commented in the House of Lords:

> Faith schools have an excellent track record on community cohesion. I attended only last week the Church of England's Living Well Together conference, which brought together students, teachers, faith leaders and others to share ideas about how we live well together and promote peaceful coexistence. I was very impressed by what the Church of England is doing to promote these discussions within schools. (Hansard 2015)

What follows is a distillation of feedback from the day. Although the feedback is, of course, important, the process of generating the ideas and preparing them for presentation is the foundation for enabling delegates to take the ideas of how to enable living well together back to their own settings. In a sense the journey is more formative than the destination.

Some central observations from the London day conference would be the following:

» Living well together requires certain dispositions, such as being open-minded, respectful of difference, honest, compassionate, welcoming, secure in personal (and corporate) identity, welcoming and accepting of others and a good sense of humour.

» The skills needed to enable self and others to live well together include empathy, listening, the ability to treat others impartially and modelling dialogue.

» Religious faith helps living well together, because:

  » It helps you to think beyond yourself, enabling you to look at the world without always having yourself at the centre.

» It helps you understand different morals and teachings; serious study of a variety of religious traditions reveals commonalities, including teachings about compassion and community.

» It encourages virtues such as compassion, hospitality and neighbourliness.

» It can lead to an increase in community cohesion.

» Religious faith can hinder living well together, because:

   » People in a particular religious tradition may be limited by ignorance and fear. They may have a sense of their own innate superiority or a self-understanding that because they have exclusive access to the truth, everyone else is inferior.

   » Religious institutions can paralyse followers of a particular religious faith or get caught up in defending self-interest.

   » The baggage of history can be a challenge for forming relations in the present.

   » The media can report complex religious problems over-simplistically or inaccurately.

The delegates at the London day conference suggested the following are essential components that should be taught to encourage living well together. The key skills identified included: emotional intelligence; the ability to facilitate discussion; the resilience to cope with challenges and disappointment; critical thinking and the ability to discern and question; and good communication skills and mediation skills. The topic of identity was argued to be central; if we are to live well together, then we must know ourselves and others. This would include teaching about self-value and self-awareness, as well as improving abilities of self-regulation. More generally, delegates argued that there is a need for improved religious literacy, including discerning the core values/shared values of the different religious traditions. This does not preclude discussing differences and debating what stances and attitudes are unacceptable in modern British society.

The overwhelming opinion of all delegates was that living well together was not a discrete subject that could be taught in an hour once a week, but rather a disposition that must be integrated through the whole curriculum. Delegates suggested that there is scope for in- and out-of-school clubs and activities and holiday clubs that promote the ideal of living well together. It was also noted that how children are welcomed into the school (both as new arrivals and on a day-to-day basis) is important for modelling living well together.

Having said that, delegates also recognised that living well together cannot be solely taught as a discrete subject; there is a particular place for quality religious education, personal, social, health and economic education, citizenship and British values teaching, and a corresponding need for development of resources and expertise in this area. But these subjects cannot solve the issue in isolation. A greater grasp of world history, for example, is a necessary precursor to understanding the complexities of modern geopolitics.

As with the question of 'when', the question of 'where' living well together should be taught was given a wide-ranging answer. In the words of one delegate: 'It should suffuse the school.' The conference suggested that all teachers across the curriculum must have the skills to facilitate children discussing their differences and commonalities. They argued for Department for Education investment in these skills so that teachers feel confident to spot opportunities to promote discussion of interfaith issues.

It was also suggested that living well together must be promoted by school leadership, the school ethos and shared values. Delegates argued that it was important to create appropriate time and space for things to happen. They suggested that fostering living well together requires a sustained and natural approach, not just an intervention. This therefore requires Ofsted to recognise that this is a long-term and committed process.

Delegates at the London day conference suggested that teaching living well together must be a whole school issue. This means training, because it would be best taught by theologically literate teachers, in conjunction with inspirational faith visitors. Having the 'right' visitors was argued to be of crucial importance, and it was also recognised that both parents and children could contribute to mutual self-understanding. There was a suggestion of the need for local co-ordination and commissioning of effective interfaith educators.

A number of strategies for teaching living well together were suggested, notably that teaching should be experiential, not just theoretical. This could be classroom based and also include visits. Teachers must be skilled at managing dialogue well and not closing down discussion. They should confidently and compassionately challenge the assumptions and prejudices of all participants. Teachers must be confident enough to risk discussion of difficult areas and enable children to discuss and question. Classroom-based learning might include meeting with inspirational faith leaders who embody respect for others. Going out into the community, for social action projects such as Sewa Day, Mitzvah Day or Sadaqa Day, was also an important component. Celebrating festivals and differing lifestyles, either through visitors coming to school or through class trips, was another key component. Finally, exchanges with other schools or links with different places of worship and community action would be valuable.

Three further Living Well Together conferences were conducted in 2016. One in March 2016, held in Leicester, involved pupils from both Year 6 and Years 12 and 13. Two further conferences were held in November 2016, one in Leicester for pupils in Years 12 and 13 and one in Southwell for pupils in Year 6. The feedback from the conferences was broadly similar to that noted above. These additional conferences allowed for further refining of the framework employed to facilitate discussion, and confirmed the organisers' hunch that a framework is necessary for ensuring good outcomes. The conferences involving pupils in Year 6 (aged 10 and 11) demonstrated that young pupils are perfectly capable of having mature conversations about difference with complete strangers. Finally, the popularity of the conferences is an indication that there is a real interest within school communities for help in having discussions about how we live well together with our differences.

CASE STUDY 2.2: TRAINING FOR PUBLIC SECTOR ORGANISATIONS

RIAZ RAVAT

I am the deputy director of the St Philip's Centre, heading up the corporate training arm of the organisation. Since the early days of the Centre, the charity has delivered a range of religious literacy training to many public sector bodies including the police and local authorities. More sporadic courses have been run for others such as Leicestershire Fire & Rescue Service, Leicester City Clinical Commissioning Group and for city schools' religious education leads via Leicester City Council.

However, our training for all new police recruits at Leicestershire Police (formerly Leicestershire Constabulary) has continued for a much longer period. Despite the peaks and troughs of recruitment cycles, we have remained a staple part of the force's induction diet. In the early days, delegates undertook a foundation degree in community policing via De Montfort University. More recently, participants complete the same qualification albeit via an internally accredited offer.

Many hundreds of police officers have sampled the St Philip's Centre experience. All our public sector training courses are rooted in authenticity and encounter. The St Philip's Centre is the responsible body but works in partnership with colleagues from the faith communities to deliver the quality 'product'. Excellence and quality means that when delegates wish to learn about Hindus, they meet a Hindu. When they learn about Judaism, they meet a Jew. It is more robust and credible to meet and learn directly. It is also made clear to delegates that they are meeting one person who lives and breathes that particular faith and is active in their community. However, it is also made clear that they are one voice amongst many. Our training participants are also not 'punished via PowerPoint'. In a world of virtual communications, our approach is one of face-to-face encounter.

A typical training day would include a 'Facts of Faiths Game', where the large group is split into teams and take part in a competitive card game exercise. The winning team is awarded a prize! This is followed by an overview of 'Religions & Beliefs in the UK', including data from the Census/Office for National Statistics. The next stage is the 'round robin' session where participants are split back into their teams and spend approximately 20 minutes with a faith practitioner on a rotational basis. They answer anonymous questions written by delegates earlier on in the day. Rather than imparting information to those attending, the 'round robin' directly poses questions related to world issues or workplace challenges. So, for example, rather than a question about how many times in a day Muslims pray, the question is likely to be: 'How can I as a line manager facilitate appropriate time off for prayer whilst ensuring business needs are fully met without compromising other aspects of the company?'

A session titled 'Case Studies' will involve groups assessing a potential or real-life example of a difficulty where solutions and, more importantly, approaches need to be assessed. In the case of the police, this will include how to respond in case of an attack on a place of worship and the resulting rumour mill about the alleged perpetrators. Finally, the day ends with a visit to a place of worship so that the day is brought together in a different setting where hospitality and welcome are the order of the day. This is also an opportunity to learn in more detail from another religion belief.

This recipe has worked very successfully for many years. When I began working at the St Philip's Centre, some of the public sector courses had a strongly academic flavour, where the reality on the ground was often missing. In addition, plenary sessions often led to hesitancy from the floor to ask questions or indeed an over-dominance of replies from questions posed to one faith over another. There is a method to our training offer, and repeated evaluations show very high levels of satisfaction. However, the challenge is that whilst many have taken on the introductory-level programme, many public sector institutions have not freed up staff to undertake the intermediate level. This is, 6 to 12 months on, a programme to identify how practice has been shaped or where new examples are shared for mutual assessment. Part of this is down to budgets but also to organisational cultures where the bare minimum is delivered.

Understanding and providing services for diverse communities in a challenging context cannot be achieved in one day. This is why the approach taken by the army through the Seventh Brigade and the 158 Regiment Royal Logistic Corps (RLC) is one which is long term and rooted in relationship building. The army's training is complemented by their own named staff member, given a sole remit of connecting with communities and offering opportunities such as leadership and development training for young people in faith venues. This begins to reposition the narrative between communities and the armed services, which is crucial.

One such example was during the visit of the Rt Hon Earl Howe to Crown Hills Community College in Leicester in February 2016, when the Armed Forces Muslim Association highlighted the Muslim contribution to the British Army in the First and Second World Wars. Many Muslims lost their lives, including Khudadad Khan, the first Muslim solider to receive the Victoria Cross, with Lord Ahmad of Wimbledon, the previous communities minister, hailing his 'exceptional loyalty, courage and determination in Britain's fight for freedom' (Malnick 2014). However, it was apparent that many of the children attending the school were not aware of this fact, which they deemed to be positive. Needless to say, there would be similar responses to other war heroes from other faiths too. Therefore, for the armed forces, understanding and appreciating history is an important part of their particular narrative of encounter. However, such narratives are not always universally settled. For example, the narrative of the relationship for sections of the black community in London and the Metropolitan Police is still dominated by the tragedy of Stephen Lawrence's murder. Learning from history to carve out new connections is key.

Recruiting from ethnic or religious minority communities, to ensure services are reflective of the areas they serve, remains a key challenge to public sector bodies despite some of the progress made. In particular, at senior management level, whether local authority, NHS, police, armed services, fire service or educational institution, there is no doubt that there are recruitment difficulties and, even if at entry level the barriers are broken, the further up the chain the less reflective they are of their respective areas. This is a significant concern, and a welcome development has been the call by Prime Minister Theresa May to order a Cabinet Office 'review into how ethnic minorities and white working class people are treated by public services such as the NHS, schools, police and the courts' (BBC 2016b). The inclusion of 'white working class' is vital in the wider context of integration and inclusion in society. How public bodies respond to the issues posed remains to be seen.

Clearly this is not a problem confined to public bodies, with the private sector also needing to reflect on its own challenges. For example, how many bank or building society boards could be said to be reflective of UK society?

3

ENCOUNTER

TOM WILSON

A group of committed Christians sat at the back of the mosque. Some were ordained, others were not, but all were active in ministry in their own church context. There were university chaplains, lay pioneer ministers, and representatives of both the Anglican and Methodist churches. All were taking part in Christian Engagement with a Multi-Faith World, a two-day programme of encounter and reflection, one of the St Philip's Centre staples. We had come to observe *zuhr*, the prayer during the middle of the day. It was a Wednesday afternoon, the mosque was in a primarily residential area, and I was not expecting great crowds. As I would normally do for such a visit, I made sure we were early, so that everyone was seated out of the way, and they could observe what happened.

Prayers were scheduled for 1:30pm, and we had arrived at 1:20pm. There were very few people in the hall at this stage, but some were sitting reading quietly or offering personal prayers. The *azan*, the call to prayer, was made, and the room sprang into life as men walked purposefully to the front of the hall, forming lines and preparing to pray. The imam began the prayers, but still people came; throughout the whole of the prayer time, more and more individuals came, some only just joining the final line as the prayer finished. Some then headed straight for the door, others found space to complete their prayers individually. We stayed for just a few more minutes, before also heading for the exit. Once we returned to the Centre, we reflected on what we had seen. There followed the expected questions about why it was that not everyone was present at 1:30pm in time for the start of prayers. Questions about what those who came in late would do, how they completed their obligation, where and when ablution took place and so forth. We then discussed what the Christians had encountered after the formal end of the prayer time. The men had had a much more positive experience; many of those exiting the prayer hall had come over to shake hands with them, offering a word of greeting. A few of the Christians had even managed to exchange greetings in Arabic: *as-salam allaykum* and the reply *wa allaykum salam* ('peace be with you' and the reply 'and peace be with you').

Some of the women on the course reported a more negative experience. No one had offered to shake hands with them. There had been some polite nods, the smile of friendship. But no possibility of physical contact. For some of the women, who had encountered sexism and discrimination in their own religious settings, this was a complicated area to reflect upon. We discussed cultural and religious differences, expectations and desires around purity, friendship and what it was appropriate to expect of someone very different but still a fellow British citizen. For some conservative Muslims, who have strong beliefs about separation of men and women, shaking hands with a woman who is not a relative would be both culturally improper and religiously questionable. However, what is meant as an exercise in preserving religious purity and maintaining appropriate decorum is experienced as rejection and even as latent misogyny. An encounter with difference caused serious reflection amongst everyone taking part in that course.

Sometimes world views can be so different that we do not realise how other people receive us if we do not have the courage to ask honest questions and talk openly about how we feel. One of the aims of much of the work that the St Philip's Centre does is to enable people to encounter difference and to reflect clearly and honestly on what that encounter means. In discussing the example of handshaking given above, one of the participants in the discussion pointed out the different cultural expectations within white British culture in the UK. In some sections of society, an air kiss or a kiss on one cheek would be expected if a man greets a woman. In other sections of society, it might be a hug or it might be a handshake. There are no clear, hard and fast rules for exactly what type of contact is appropriate. Faced with such complexity, this individual went on, is it any wonder that some people decided that no contact is the best option? This observation is an accurate one. There is a wide variety of views as to how men and women should greet each other within British society, but the general expectation is of proactive engagement, not distancing. Having encountered something very different, these Christians had to decide how they came to terms with this difference.

I took a different group to visit a gurdwara. They were also on an experience and reflection programme, this time over a whole weekend. The gurdwara is a busy place on a Saturday. Although some of the regular weekday activities do not run, there are far more visitors, as people who do not have time to gather during the week take advantage of the relative freedom of the weekend. The visitors formed a large group, over 30 strong, and we were all white. It was obvious we were visitors, and the body language of some within the group suggested clearly that they were somewhat outside of their comfort zones. We waited for quite a while for our host. The visit was booked, and I had spoken with him about it. I knew he would come, but sometimes the best-laid plans do not turn out exactly as you hope and you have to wait. We did wait, for about 30 minutes.

Personally, I found this a great opportunity to chat with some of the participants, find out what they had thought of the programme so far, answer some questions and give them an opportunity to observe the hustle and bustle of a gurdwara over a Saturday lunchtime. For some on the course it was an interminably long, anxiety-inducing wait. When we had been liaising with the programme organiser, she had commented on the need for precise timings in the schedule for the weekend. I had obliged, but we had also agreed that these timings would, in practice, be very approximate – and so it proved. Our guide did arrive, showed us round, and all taking part had an opportunity for learning and also for refreshment, as we took *langar* (the free community meal served at most gurdwaras).

Here we were encountering a primarily cultural difference around expectations of what 'arrival at 1pm' meant in terms of the precise time at which things took place. Culture and religion are, of course, both separate and also intricately inter-related. In the case of worship at a gurdwara, it is possible for individuals to attend whenever it is open for private devotion and also for them to come to only some, or all, of the public events, which may last for ten hours or more. The precise timing equivalent of a Western church service does not quite translate into the corporate worshipping life of a gurdwara. The Christians had to reflect on what constituted appropriate religious worship as well as cultural expectations around time.

Any meeting between two people is an encounter with difference. Sometimes these differences are relatively modest, especially if the people come from the same cultural context and share a similar world view. At other times the differences are of greater significance. The St Philip's Centre facilitates encounters between difference but does not necessarily aim for people to reach compromise over those differences. We do not see our role as being brokers of agreement, especially of the lowest common denominator type of agreement that minimises differences to such an extent that distinct identity is lost. Rather than telling people what to think or believe, our aim is to enable people to discover the rich diversity of views that exist in Britain today and to help individuals reflect on their own beliefs in the light of what others think.

An important point to bear in mind when facilitating encounters is that often the most contentious differences are those which exist within a particular faith tradition rather than those which exist between faith traditions. Thus, for example, members of the Orthodox and Progressive Jewish communities may engage in far more robust discussion about what constitutes authentic Judaism. To cite another example, members of the ISKCON (International Society for Krishna Consciousness, or Hare Krishna) movement are sometimes dismissed by other Hindus as not presenting an authentic voice of Hinduism. Intrafaith encounter, we often say, is in fact far more complex than interfaith encounter. This topic is picked up in the next chapter.

The main aim of any encounter is that it becomes a stimulus for learning and reflection, that it is a chance for understanding to develop. One can look both to learn about the religious viewpoints of other people and also to get a clearer sense of your own religious views. In what follows, we outline the challenges that preclude against such learning taking place.

How to best facilitate encounter?

Encounters with difference work best when all those involved genuinely want to do precisely that: encounter difference. Some of the training that the St Philip's Centre organises can be compulsory for those participating. Youth workers may have to take part in an interfaith encounter module as part of their training, or members of the armed forces may be told by their commanding officer that they are going to spend the day attending training on diversity, to give just two examples. Compulsory training is not always willingly received and there may be a reluctance to genuinely engage. This reluctance may stem from fear, grounded or otherwise, that the by-product of encounter will be forced change, spiritual contamination, an uncomfortable time or maybe simply an expectation that the main encounter will be with boredom. If people do not want a productive encounter, invariably they do not have one, although skilled faith practitioners, used to engaging with those who have some reluctance about encounter, can overcome these barriers.

It is important to recognise that these fears exist, even if they are not explicitly addressed. Proper briefing, including a clear explanation of what participants will be expected to do, how they should behave and what they should wear, is an essential prerequisite for any encounter. Our normal practice would be to send a short briefing document to all participants on courses that involve visits to places of worship, explaining general expectations of behaviour in a place of worship and dress codes in particular. Practical details must receive appropriate attention, ensuring participants on visits know where they need to be and when. If people travel in their own cars, then the challenge of navigating unfamiliar areas, finding parking and so forth can detract from the experience. As far as possible we endeavour to arrange group transportation so that participants can concentrate on the encounters without worrying about how to get there. Furthermore, allowing participants to express anxiety, either verbally or through forming a 'human rainbow', enables acknowledgement of concerns without the need for in-depth discussion.[1]

The precise place of worship visited and the attitude of the guide around that place of worship are also crucial. On a practical level, issues such as parking, accessibility of the place of worship, heating and so forth must all be considered. Pragmatic reality may mean that conditions are less than ideal, but there is often some leeway. Of greater importance is the attitude of the guide. A good guide will have the aim of facilitating encounter; a bad one will be thinking in terms of promulgation of a party line, or even of conversion. When the St Philip's Centre selects people to act as guides around places of worship, we are looking for people who are confident in their own faith, but at the same time respect the different faith traditions of those who are visiting them. The confidence is important, because people should not be expected to apologise for the views they hold, nor feel under pressure to present an airbrushed view of their religious community. We want our course participants to have an encounter with the reality of religious faith as lived out in a particular community. Those who have an appropriate confidence in their own beliefs are able to explain them to people who think differently, tackling controversial topics in a constructive manner, which opens up conversation rather than closing it down. By contrast, those who are looking to promulgate or convert can adopt

---

1   Before going on visits to places of worship, I might ask course participants to form a 'human rainbow', positioning themselves between two alternatives, such as 'I am really excited to visit these places of worship' and 'I am really dreading visiting these places of worship'. This allows us to acknowledge the spectrum of views present without it becoming an overly wordy or invasive exercise.

a more confrontational approach to introducing their faith community, which rarely leads to a productive encounter. Some examples may illustrate the point. One of the guides we regularly use within the Jewish community is clear in explaining the *kashrut* (Jewish dietary) laws. He is equally clear in explaining the Orthodox Jewish understanding of the separation of men and women during worship, that a rabbi in his tradition should be male and the reasons why some within the Orthodox Jewish community do not engage with all sections of civil society, such as the LGBT community. Many of those who hear these explanations disagree with him about the appropriateness of these views, but the object of the exercise is not to force agreement but to facilitate encounter that can lead to understanding and a greater appreciation both of the fact that people hold different views and also their reasons for holding them. He is someone who is confident but not confrontational, whose presentations open up conversation and facilitate positive encounters.

By contrast, a guide within a different community, who is no longer used by the Centre, tended to use visits as an opportunity to persuade course participants of the correctness of his own views and the error of theirs. Those who disagreed were not given opportunities to question or debate, but rather simply told they were incorrect. These encounters were quite counter-productive, reinforcing negative stereotypes and acting as barriers to learning. The particular challenge for an organisation such as the St Philip's Centre is that if the nominated guide to a particular place of worship follows these negative actions, it can be better to no longer take visitors to that place of worship. We are not in a position to tell other communities who they should put forward as their spokespeople; we can only offer advice and training where appropriate.

Some may argue that a negative encounter can still be a productive one, enabling learning to take place. This is true, to some extent, but it depends on the audience. The St Philip's Centre believes that positive encounters are crucial for those who are making their first steps into engagement with people of other faiths, and especially for the young. Thus, if we are facilitating a school party visiting a place of worship, or meeting with faith community leaders, we ensure that they are people able to facilitate positive encounters. More experienced course participants, especially those whose role includes working with diverse sections of society, can benefit from the more negative encounters, if only to enable them to understand the scale of the challenge that exists in facilitating the positive integration of all sections of society. We would therefore not, for example, introduce young children to the strong differences of opinion there are between some Sunni and Shi'a Muslims, but we might ensure that church leaders understood the nuances of these debates.

Our main aim in facilitating encounters is therefore to look for people who understand their own tradition well, who have enough self-awareness to be able to self-manage in the face of complex, potentially hostile, questioning, and who are looking to learn as well as to teach within the encounter. If such qualities are required of the faith practitioners we work with, then we must also expect a similar attitude of those participating in the courses that we run.

Course participants are expected to approach encounters in as openminded a manner as possible. We do not necessarily expect anyone to radically change their views as a result of such encounters, but it is helpful if they are open to the possibility of change and also to recognising that they have much to learn. A respect for the sincere convictions and traditions of others is important, exemplified in a willingness to remove shoes, wear head coverings, eat curry while sitting on the floor and receive food that has been offered to a *murti* (Hindu religious image), which are some examples of the types of behaviour required of course participants.

This final example can be problematic to some, whose own sincere religious convictions prohibit the worship of idols and the receipt of anything offered to those idols. Encountering this difference, recognising that what the Abrahamic faiths refer to as idol worship may not be what the Hindu tradition understands by a *murti*, leads to a rich conversation when all can learn and grow. But such conversations require courage; people need to find the right words to articulate their experience, to explain what they think is happening and invite others to present an alternative perspective. I can remember on a number of occasions facilitating visits to a Hindu *mandir* and asking on behalf of course participants why certain symbols were present. The visitors saw a Nazi symbol, but for the worshipping community, the *svastika* indicates symmetry, and is a sacred and auspicious sign.

CASE STUDY 3.1: ARMED FORCES

The St Philip's Centre has been developing a working relationship with the British armed forces since the summer of 2015. In addition to a number of engagement activities, we have hosted two visits to Leicester from the Rt Hon Earl Howe, minister of state for the Ministry of Defence and deputy leader of the House of Lords. The main aim of these visits was to help the different faith communities and the armed forces to encounter each other and to 'normalise' one another, following a policy of engagement first, recruitment later. There is a great deal of misunderstanding and misinformation on all sides, and the St Philip's Centre's aim has been primarily for encounters that allow greater understanding to develop.

From the perspective of the armed forces, they exist to protect and serve all British citizens and, indeed, when on international deployment to protect and serve the local community where they are based, in so far as that aim is compatible with their mission. There is an understanding that their presence in a community is a positive thing and that a career in the armed forces is a good option for anyone looking for a challenging, but rewarding, life. Whilst they recognise that there are some who have a different perspective, the detail of this is not widely understood. Coupled with a directive from the former Prime Minister David Cameron's office that by 2020 the armed forces should have at least 10 per cent of their membership drawn from minority ethnic communities, the imperative to engage has become even greater.

The armed forces face a significant challenge in ensuring that the faith of those serving with them reflects the faith make-up of the population of the United Kingdom as a whole. Table 3.1 sets out the disparity (Census 2011 n.d.; Ministry of Defence 2014, 2016).

As Table 3.1 indicates, the significant differences are, first, the greater proportion of Christians in the armed forces than the general population and, second, the greater proportion of Muslims in the general population than in the armed forces. Given the general population figures are five years older than the latest military data, it is likely that both of these gaps are in fact greater than these figures suggest. The armed forces still have some ground to make up in relation to the Jewish, Sikh and Hindu populations, but by far the greatest challenge comes in relating to the Muslim community.

Table 3.1 Religious affiliation in the armed forces compared with the general public

	Armed forces April 2012		Armed forces April 2016		2011 Census[1]
	Number	Percentage[2]	Number	Percentage	Percentage
Buddhist	520	0.3	690	0.5	0.4
Christian	148,550	83.5	113,250	75.5	59.3
Christian Tradition[3]	260	0.1	200	0.1	0.1
Hindu	820	0.5	1,020	0.7	1.5
Judaism	80	–	70	–	0.5
Muslim	650	0.4	520	0.3	4.8
Sikh	130	0.1	160	0.1	0.8
Other Religions[4]	820	0.5	790	0.5	0.3
No Religion	26,180	14.7	33,380	22.2	25.1
Unknown	1 800	n/a	900	n/a	7.2

Notes:

1 Although these figures are out of date compared to the armed forces figures, they are the most recent national figures. The more recent Social Attitudes Surveys are based on much smaller population samples.

2 Calculated as a percentage of those who declared a religion.

3 'Christian Tradition' includes personnel declaring as: Christian Tradition, Christian Scientist, Church of Jesus Christ of Latter-Day Saints (Mormon), Jehovah's Witness, Unitarian and Other Christian Tradition.

4 'Other Religions' includes personnel declaring as: Druid, Pagan, Rastafarian, Spiritualist, Zoroastrian (Parsee), Wicca, Baha'i and Other Religions.

Our experience suggests that actually the armed forces are quite knowledgeable about religion and belief. On our first training day for mid-ranking and senior officers, the winning team in the 'Facts of Faiths' game got the highest score ever achieved by a public sector organisation. Many of the officers who participated in the course could tell stories of encounters with people of different faiths from their deployments around the world. Moreover, the six core army values (courage, discipline, respect for others, integrity, loyalty and selfless commitment) have many resonances with religious beliefs. However, if the armed forces have good knowledge about faith, then why are the faith communities so reluctant to serve with them?

There are a wide range of Christian views about the armed forces, from those who are complete pacifists and oppose all military action, to those who are Christians and have a strong sense of calling to the armed forces. But most Christians fall somewhere in between these two. One Christian we spoke with said:

> The armed forces are a reluctant necessity, and most people who serve are dedicated, committed and prepared to sacrifice their own life in order that others might live. But, our world is complex and messy, and so sometimes we get it wrong, and sometimes we rely on power and fighting before we have exhausted love; and sometimes you have to fight in order to love and protect, but we must never do that for our own gain.

For the Jewish community in the UK, being in the armed forces is simply not high on the list of possible career options. This is partly because of a desire to avoid violence (as even the Israeli army defines itself as a self-defence force, not an offensive force). Orthodox Jews would avoid the armed forces particularly because of the challenge of being able to observe Shabbat.[2] The *kashrut* (food) laws are also a challenge, but this is easier to accommodate, as specific allowances can be made. Having said that, it is possible that, although provision is made in theory, in practice in the field

---

2   There are two central elements to Shabbat. First, remembrance of the divine creation of the world and liberation from slavery in Egypt and, second, observance of the command to refrain from *melachah*, creative or controlling activity, normally termed 'work'.

this may not always be realised. The only exception would be that some Jews might find it acceptable to take on jobs involving saving a life, so training as a doctor or nurse within the armed forces might be fine for some. Similarly, parents in the Hindu community simply do not encourage their children to join the armed forces, as ultimately there is a possibility of their being involved in armed combat. When they are engaged in discussion about this, Hindus do recognise that there are many career paths within the armed forces that do not include being on the front line, but the option of an armed forces career is not in the consciousness of most Hindus because of the heavy emphasis on combat. This is evident in so many of the media communications produced by the armed forces. This may well be partly because those whose parents came to the UK as migrants have strong aspirations to better themselves materially and so focus on financially rewarding careers as accountants, doctors, dentists and the like. A further reason is the lack of role models. There are very few Hindus visible in the armed forces.

The Sikh community, by contrast, do have a long tradition of involvement with the armed forces and have gone about marking their contributions during the First and Second World Wars. However, they too are few in number in the current armed forces but have a stronger starting point to begin to turn the tide. Interest in a career in the armed forces may also develop over time. The first generation of migrants to the UK was concerned primarily with simple survival. Many arrived with little or no financial resources, and focused heavily on establishing themselves within the UK. As such their focus was very much on their immediate family. Their children moved from survival to seeking to establish financial security, and as such focused on economically beneficial, 'safer' careers, such as accountancy or medicine. Their children, the grandchildren of the first migrants, are those who are looking for success, and are more open to taking risks and establishing careers in less traditional pathways. This may well include the armed forces, but only time will tell.

Reservations within the Muslim community concerning the armed forces have been fuelled in recent years, through the involvement of the British armed forces in conflicts in Syria, Iraq and Afghanistan. Some Muslims understand these conflicts primarily, or indeed exclusively, as a war on Islam and hence are completely opposed to any encounter with British military personnel. For others, while they may not see things in such extreme terms, the possibility of being involved in a combat situation facing other Muslims is enough to dissuade them from the possibility of a military career. It should also be noted, however, that there are Muslims in the British armed forces who primarily see themselves as being loyal British citizens serving their country.

Our work with the armed forces is not restricted to the British Army. Since 2012 we have annually hosted an international delegation of very senior military figures via the Royal College of Defence Studies – the prestigious institution for 'officers of the Armed Forces and equivalent civil servants who have the potential to reach the highest ranks and who must therefore understand and be comfortable working at the strategic level in a cross-government and international environment' (Defence Academy n.d.).

CASE STUDY 3.2: MEDICAL ETHICS: BEGINNING AND END OF LIFE ISSUES

The St Philip's Centre runs a number of different encounter programmes for medical professionals, including a course for those training to be doctors and for those involved in GP surgeries. These courses focus on developing understanding of how issues of religion and belief impact medical professionals. Two examples will illustrate the point from a religious perspective. First, one of the core beliefs within Sikhism is that an *Amritdhari* Sikh will not cut his or her hair. This poses a problem for some forms of surgery that may require hair to be shaved. Second, Jehovah's Witnesses are not allowed to receive blood transfusions and so are unable to undergo some surgical procedures or even receive some lifesaving treatments at times of trauma. Sometimes the urgency of a medical procedure takes priority over religious expectations. Many places of worship require those visiting to remove their shoes, but does a paramedic responding to an emergency call for someone who has had a heart attack have time to stop and remove shoes?

In this case study, an overview of beginning and end of life issues from the perspective of six major world faiths discusses questions such as 'When does life begin?', 'Is contraception acceptable?' and 'Is euthanasia ever permissible?'

Most religious traditions have strong teaching about the sanctity of life. The precise reasoning varies between religious traditions but, if God is viewed as creator, there follows teaching about divine sovereignty over life, and hence opposition to abortion. There is variation between and within religions as to whether abortion is ever permissible (and what forms of contraception, if any, are acceptable), but a general consensus that abortion should only take place in very limited circumstances. Although a particular religious tradition may have a stated teaching on this topic, that does not necessarily mean that everyone who identifies as a member of that tradition will actually follow that teaching. The official position of the Roman Catholic Church, for example, is that all artificial forms of contraception are forbidden, as they are seen as human attempts to limit divine sovereignty over procreation. But the reality is that many Roman Catholic women do take contraceptive pills. This difference between lived and doctrinal religion can also manifest itself in national politics. In countries where a particular faith is dominant, the law of the land may also take a particular view with which many do not agree. A recent example is of Poland trying to push through an anti-abortion law, supported by the Catholic Church, which would prohibit abortion even in cases of rape or incest. But in October 2016 thousands of women boycotted work, wore black and protested in the streets to express their anger at this proposed law (BBC 2016c). The official (doctrinal) teaching of a religion may vary greatly from the lived day-to-day practice. Any encounter around this issue must therefore pay attention to both the official teaching and the lived practice of any particular faith community.

Opinion is equally divided about end of life issues. As with abortion, people of faith tend to be united in opposition to euthanasia, but once the complexities of the debate are explored, much more nuanced positions emerge. Even those who are strong advocates of palliative care until death are clear that if hastened death is a side effect of pain control, then it does not count as euthanasia. Moreover, people of faith debate whether physician-assisted suicide is acceptable in cases of terminal illness, with some seeing it as a slippery slope to social coercion in favour of euthanasia or even eugenics, while others see it as an appropriate way to exercise love and compassion to those in unbearable pain.

The religions being examined in this case study fall broadly into two camps: the Abrahamic traditions (Judaism, Christianity, Islam) and the Indian traditions (Hinduism, Jainism, Buddhism, Sikhism). It will be necessary to define some terms before examining each faith alphabetically in turn, so that what is meant by 'end of life' and 'beginning of life' issues is clear. The aim of this case study is to be both informative and thought-provoking, triggering questions for discussion amongst individuals who are trying to understand the sanctity of life from various faith perspectives.

Definition of terms

'The sanctity of life' is a shorthand for how life is regarded as sacred or special, with particular reference to religious ideas. This most obviously covers medical ethical issues such as abortion, different types of euthanasia (potentially including a 'do not resuscitate' notice) and contraception, as well as religious practices such as funeral rites and rituals such as baptism or naming ceremonies, but the case study only looks at the former.

'Beginning of life' often hinges around philosophical ideas of when life begins, whether at the moment of conception, a certain number of weeks into pregnancy or even once a child is actually born. 'End of life', on the other hand, is partly reliant on religious belief about what happens when we die. Broadly speaking, the Abrahamic traditions believe that there is a single earthly life, followed by judgement, whereas the Indian traditions believe in reincarnation: something non-bodily lives on and is trapped in the wheel of *samsara* until liberation is achieved. Often, achieving human life is seen as a rare or difficult opportunity and therefore not to be wasted. That said, although the body may just be a vehicle for the soul or an imprint, that does not mean disposal of a human body is taken any less seriously. There may also be issues for people of different faiths around organ donation, post-mortems and the relative merits of burial and cremation, although rituals after death are not discussed here.

Examining each faith
Buddhism

The Five Precepts for Buddhists are: not to kill or injure living creatures (*ahimsa* – non-violence); not to take what has not been given; to avoid misconduct in sensual matters; to abstain from false speech; and not to take intoxicants.

The concept of *ahimsa* (the first precept) is key when discussing issues such as abortion and euthanasia: if killing 'a living creature' is prohibited, then on the basis of the Five Precepts Buddhists would not permit abortion or euthanasia, which are both deliberate terminations of life. However, there is no single Buddhist view on abortion or voluntary euthanasia. While some see it as the deliberate end of life (and therefore a violent act), other Buddhists might see it as necessary, if, for example, the mother's life is in danger or because of immense suffering. The Dalai Lama (who speaks for a particular school of Tibetan Buddhism) once commented that 'I think abortion should be approved or disapproved according to each circumstance' (Dreifus 1993). That said, many Buddhists believe that life begins at conception, and therefore that there may be karmic imbalance for those performing abortions or permitting them, and also for the unborn foetus. In Japan, where abortion is a form of birth control, some Buddhists 'who have had an abortion make offerings to Jizo, the god of lost travellers and children. They believe that Jizo will steward the child until it is reborn in another incarnation.' This is a particular modern reaction to abortion; the offerings take part in a memorial service, but some scholars have criticised this ritual for 'manipulation of parental guilt' (BBC 2009a).

What of birth control and the use of contraception? In Buddhist thought there is a difference between *preventing* and *stopping*. This is because of the generally agreed Buddhist view that life begins at conception; therefore, if an egg has been fertilised but is stopped from implantation by birth control methods such as an IUD, that is wrong. But methods such as condoms, which prevent fertilisation in the first place, are acceptable. The Third Precept, of avoiding misconduct in sensual matters, is relevant here, as this prohibits promiscuity. Therefore, birth control should not be used just so a person can be promiscuous, a view all the faith traditions explored in this case study would share. Organ donation after death is generally permissible; it may merit *karma* for the dead person. Also, it may help to relieve the suffering of many others. From that perspective, organ donation is a positive thing to do. However, 'followers of Tibetan Buddhism believe the consciousness may stay in the body for some time after the breath has stopped', and this has clear implications for organ donation (BBC 2009b).

Christianity

Christianity comprises a huge variety of denominations, liberal and conservative approaches and personal convictions. Throughout this section I will try to balance 'official' denominational teaching with the opinions of ordinary Christians, taking two of the largest Christian denominations (Roman Catholicism and the Anglican Communion) as examples.

Many Catholics rigorously follow the teachings and edicts of the Pope, the head of the Catholic Church. This would include only using the rhythm/natural method of contraception. This is because the birth of a child is a gift from God and to prevent that in any way would be sinful. In Catholic countries such as Ireland and Brazil, abortions are banned. In Vatican City, abortion is banned absolutely – including if the birth is as a result of rape. The Society for the Protection of the Unborn Child (SPUC) is a large Catholic, pro-life campaigning organisation. That said, not all Catholics necessarily agree with the teachings of the Catholic Church regarding contraception or abortion. But even Pope Francis, considered to be fairly liberal, has referred to abortion as 'a horrific symptom of a throwaway culture' (Squires 2014).

The Anglican Communion, which has at its head the Archbishop of Canterbury, takes a slightly softer approach to abortion, although not by much. However, the laws of the countries where particular Anglican Churches find themselves also need to be taken into account here. To take the Church of England as our example, the General Synod accepts that, under some circumstances, such as if the life of the mother were in danger, abortion may be permissible. In England, abortion has to be carried out within the first 24 weeks and the Church of England encourages those who wish to have an abortion to do so as soon as possible. It is important to note here that the Church of England was instrumental in helping to bring about laws in England to allow abortions to happen, as so many women were dying as a result of backstreet (illegal) abortions.

When it comes to euthanasia, Christian teaching in general prohibits voluntary euthanasia. This is because it is believed that a person is made in the image of God. Life is a gift from God; no human being has the authority to end life. Rather, emphasis should be put on better palliative care and making a person as comfortable as possible towards the end of their life.

What of organ donation? It is not only accepted but actively encouraged by Christian denominations, including most Protestant churches, the Roman Catholic Church and Eastern Orthodox Christianity. Not only is it a compassionate act, it also sits well with key biblical verses such as John 15.13: 'greater love has no one than this: to lay down one's life for one's friends'.

Hinduism

Hinduism is actually an umbrella term for a diverse range of beliefs, practices and religious traditions. There is no founder, no single authority and no central text that binds Hindus together. That said, whilst it can be difficult to tie Hindus together in terms of doctrine and practice, it is possible to generalise with some ethical issues.

Like Buddhism, the concept of *ahimsa* (non-violence) is important for many Hindus, and therefore the arguments related by Buddhists about abortion as a violent act also apply. Also, as a married couple's *dharma* (duty) involves procreation in Hinduism, abortion may be considered *adharma* (going against one's duty). Because Hindus believe in *karma* and rebirth, the human life is a precious one (the majority of Hindus believe that only humans can achieve *moksha*, or liberation, from *samsara*). There may also be karmic consequences for the aborted foetus, not just for the person who allowed or performed the abortion.

The main arguments around euthanasia stem from the concepts of *ahimsa* and *karma*. First, that voluntary euthanasia goes against the concept of non-violence, and second, that it will have effects on one's *karma* (and that of the patient). However, one argument in support of euthanasia might be that if you are helping someone in pain, then that is a good deed, and it may even be one's *dharma* or duty. A related concept is *prayopavesa* (fasting to the death). Some Hindus believe that fasting to the death is acceptable. It is considered different to suicide, because it is non-violent, and also a person can only fast to death if it is the right time for them to die. Furthermore, there are set conditions to be met: inability to perform normal bodily purification; death appears imminent or the condition is so bad that life's pleasures are nil; the decision is publicly declared; and the action must be done under community regulation (BBC 2009c).

As for organ donation, the concepts of *dharma* and *karma* suggest that to give one's organs away after death is a positive act. It brings to mind a verse from the Bhagavad Gita (2:22) about the body being 'a coat that the atman discards, before putting on another'. The body is a vehicle for the *atman* and, once the *atman* has left the body, the body really doesn't have a use, so why not donate organs that can be used to save the life of others?

Islam

For Muslims, human life is sacred and given by Allah. This view is expressed throughout the Qur'an, for example 17:33: 'Do not take life, which Allah made sacred, other than in the course of justice.' This is key to understanding ethical issues relating to the beginning and end of human life in Islam.

The question of when life begins is a contested topic among Islamic scholars, and this naturally has an impact on when (if ever) abortion is permissible. There are generally two schools of thought: life begins at 40 days, or life begins at 120 days. 'Life begins' in this case refers to when the soul (*Ruh*) enters the body. Before that, abortion is permissible because the foetus is not yet 'a living being'. However, for many Muslims life would begin at conception, and the foetus has rights from that moment forth. If the life of the mother is in danger, abortions are acceptable even after the 120-day mark. As for cases of rape/incest, unwanted pregnancy and so forth, there is debate among scholars. At the end of the day, abortion is *haram* (forbidden), but there will be cases where it is permitted (as above). This prohibition is rooted in Qur'anic verses such as 5:32: 'Whosoever has spared the life of a soul, it is as though he has spared the life of all people. Whosoever has killed a soul, it is as though he has murdered all of mankind'; and 17:32: 'Kill not your offspring for fear of poverty; it is we who provide for them and for you. Surely, killing them is a great sin.'

This issue of abortion would also apply to forms of contraception that prevent a fertilised egg implanting in the womb. However, generally, contraceptive methods that prevent fertilisation in the first place (such as condoms) are acceptable, within the context of family life – because in Islam, children are not only a gift from God but a gift within marriage.

What of end of life issues? The Qur'an indirectly prohibits both suicide and euthanasia: 'Destroy not yourselves. Surely Allah is ever merciful to you' (4:29). The complicating factor is determining what exactly constitutes euthanasia. For example, 'Many devout Muslims believe that Do Not Resuscitate (DNR) orders represent a soft form of euthanasia' (BBC 2012). There is therefore considerable variation amongst Muslims as to what is, and is not, permitted at the end of life.

There are two perspectives on organ donation: some Muslim scholars would argue that Qur'anic verses such as 'Whosoever saves a life, it would be as if he saved the life of all mankind' (5:32) clearly support the life-giving nature of organ donation. On the other hand, some scholars would argue that the human body is inviolable and donation is not (always) permissible (NHS n.d.a).

Jainism

The principle of *ahimsa* is taken extremely seriously by Jains; from not eating after sunset, so as to avoid eating tiny insects by mistake, to a Jain monk brushing the path before him, so as to limit harm. This commitment to non-violence is perhaps most noticeable in diet, but, in reality, affects everything that a Jain person does and thinks.

It is important to note that, for Jains (and for Hindus as well), attaining human life is rare, which makes it even more precious. As might be expected, life begins at conception and 'the new gross body at conception is already associated with a subtle karmic body, which determines the physical form of a living being' (Shah 1998, p.48). Unlike in the other Indian faith traditions, for Jains, *karma* is a physical substance that literally sticks to the soul. To abort the foetus not only generates *karma* for the person doing the aborting, but can have consequences for the yet-to-be-born life, whose chances of being born human in the first place were already extremely low. A Jain text, *Sutra Krutaanga*, would seem to back up a ban on abortion, as something which causes intentional harm, when it states: 'Those who kill any living being either themselves or who have it killed by someone else or support someone else who is killing, eventually increases their own enmity' (1:1:3). Furthermore, not just the act of ending life but supporting someone who ends that life increases enmity.

The same arguments about generating *karma*, and absolute commitment to *ahimsa*, can also be applied to Jain understanding of voluntary euthanasia. As in Hinduism, however, there is a process of 'fasting to the death', this time called *sallekhana*. Again, *sallekhana* is not considered to be suicide or euthanasia, because it is a non-violent act; it is 'exclusively directed towards the soul and must be performed with a sacred formula on one's lips' (Dundas 2002, p.179). Whilst a rare practice, there have been a handful of prominent cases, and William Dalrymple's interview of a Jain nun who has experienced *sallekhana*, and subsequently embraces the practice herself, is a rare insight into the reasoning and understanding behind such an act. The nun, Mataji, says that 'sallekhana is not suicide... It is quite different. Suicide is a great sin, the result of despair. But sallekhana is a triumph over death, an expression of hope' (Dalrymple 2010, p.5). On the other hand, some human rights groups think that *sallekhana* should not be allowed. Organ donation is permissible in Jainism, including the eyes.

Judaism

The sanctity of human life is important for Jewish people; 'Thou shall not kill' is one of the Ten Commandments given by God to Moses. That is not to say, however, that issues such as 'abortion' and 'assisted dying' are black and white issues for Jewish people. For example, there is the issue of whose life is more important: whilst the foetus has the right to life, the mother also has the right to life. If pregnancy or labour puts the mother's life in danger, Judaism actually necessitates that the mother's life be saved above that of the foetus (Mishna, Oholot 7:6). So, in cases such as these, abortion is permitted. To summarise Jewish positions on abortion, the abortion must be undertaken for serious reasons, usually relating to health, and it is not permitted as a form of birth control. According to one source, 'Jewish law is more lenient concerning abortions in the first forty days of pregnancy as it considers the embryo to be of relatively low value during this time' (BBC 2009d). So whilst UK law says that abortion can be carried out up to 24 weeks, in Judaism having an abortion within the first 40 days is preferable to having the procedure later on.

In terms of euthanasia and suicide, life is precious and should not be wasted. However, there are two key passages where an inference can be drawn about euthanasia. In the book of Judges, one man implores another to kill him, because he has sustained great injuries from a female assailant:

> And a certain woman threw an upper millstone upon Abimelech's head, and crushed his skull. Then he called hastily to the young man his armour-bearer, and said to him, 'Draw your sword and kill me, lest men say of me, "A woman killed him."' And his young man thrust him through, and he died. (Judges 9.53–54)

For Abimelech, it is better to die at the hands of a man than a woman, so in this case he is asking for help in dying so as to protect his honour. 2 Samuel has a similar story about protecting honour, for King Saul (who is seriously injured) orders a solider to kill him, rather than let him fall into the hands of his enemies. However, the difference in this story is that King David then has the soldier executed 'to show that euthanasia was equivalent to murder, and that the defence of superior orders was valueless' (BBC 2009d).

Organ donation is slightly more complex in Judaism; whilst it is encouraged and can be seen as a great honour in saving another person's life, issues arise over the exact point of death. Thus, 'a doctor needs irrefutable evidence that the individual is not conscious and is not likely to be so again – particularly when he or she is driven by the urgent possibility of saving another life through organ transplant' (Morgan and Lawton 1996, p.153). However, some Jewish people, and therefore rabbis from whom permission might be sought, may be less comfortable with donating organs for medical research.

Sikhism

As with all the faiths examined in this case study, human life is precious for Sikhs. Whilst medical ethical issues such as abortion and euthanasia might be considered modern issues, and therefore rarely dealt with directly in Holy Scriptures, nevertheless guidance may be found within them on issues related to the preservation of life. Verses from Guru Granth Sahib describe how prayer and penance were performed in the womb (74:16–17), and from this it can be argued that life begins at conception. Therefore, abortion would destroy a life, no matter how early the pregnancy. Generally, Sikhs are anti-abortion (although it is not discussed in the Sikh Code of Conduct).

Furthermore, life is a gift from God; presumably therefore voluntary euthanasia and suicide are rejections of the gift of human life. *Sewa* (selfless works or acts) are highly significant to Sikhs, and one suggestion is that 'the Sikh reaction to situations where people think about euthanasia would be to provide such good care that euthanasia became an unattractive option' (BBC 2009e).

And what of organ donation? To return again to the principle of *Sewa*, organ donation to save the life of another human being may be seen as a compassionate and selfless act and is therefore highly commendable. The Sikh religion teaches that life continues after death in the soul, and not the physical body. Thus Lord Singh of Wimbledon suggests that the last act of giving and helping others through organ donation is both consistent with and in the spirit of Sikh teachings (NHS n.d.b).

Summary

Beliefs about the beginning and end of life impinge upon the beliefs and practices of the world's faiths and their practitioners. To summarise the discussion: the religions examined in this case study by and large view abortion as something completely prohibited or acceptable only within special circumstances; certainly never as a form of birth control. Voluntary euthanasia is not accepted by any of the world's religions and neither is suicide, although there are two faiths, Hinduism and Jainism, which have 'fasting to the death' practices (*prayopavesa* and *sallekhana*), which some outside of those faiths might regard as a form of euthanasia or suicide.

Views on the use of contraception tend to fall into two camps: that which prohibits conception in the first place, and that which prevents a fertilised egg from implanting. In most cases, where there is a religious concern about contraception it tends to be with the latter form. However, Roman Catholicism is strict in its views that any form of contraception other than the rhythm/natural method is not to be used.

Organ donation is generally permissible, and even encouraged, within various faith communities, if it is going to save the life of another human being. This is seen as a selfless and compassionate act, and for the Indian traditions may well generate merit or *karma*. That said, the point at which life ends (which involves arguments around when the heart stops beating or when the brain stops working) can cause issues for some faith groups, such as Judaism, as can invading the 'sacredness' of the human body (such as Islam).

Such ethical issues are never straightforward, but this case study has enabled the reader to encounter a variety of views around some complex issues. The encounter should lead to greater understanding of, but not necessarily agreement with, the variety of perspectives expressed.

4

UNDERSTAND

TOM WILSON

On 12 and 13 November 2015 the Prime Minister of India, Narendra Modi, visited the UK. There was, to put it mildly, a mixed reaction to his visit from Indians living in the UK and British citizens of Indian heritage. For Hindus, Modi is a man to celebrate. He is regarded as a successful leader, a breath of fresh air, who is helping India modernise and change. The second most populous nation on earth, often described as 'the world's biggest democracy', has more than its fair share of problems with corruption and government incompetence. Modi's supporters argue that he is changing all this. He, they suggest, brings a new approach to government, an outward focus, enabling business deals to be made, bringing much needed investment into the Indian economy. The *Daily Telegraph* reported that around £10 billion in deals would be signed during this two-day visit to the UK (Fraser 2015). Modi is therefore a man to be celebrated, fêted even. On 13 November 2015, 60,000 people were in a packed Wembley Stadium to give him a rapturous welcome and applaud his efforts on behalf of India. Coaches travelled to London from many cities with large Hindu populations, including many from Leicester.

Not all of the coaches which left Leicester to go to Wembley were filled with people who supported Modi.

Some went to stand outside the stadium, to protest about the visit. Indian Sikhs and Muslims in particular have serious grievances against Modi and are not shy in voicing their views. Their concerns relate particularly to the period when Modi was chief minister of the Indian state of Gujarat. As the *Guardian* notes, on 27 February 2002, a train coach carrying Hindu pilgrims caught fire in Godhra station in Gujarat, killing 58 people. Within hours, Modi declared that the Pakistani secret services had been to blame. He then had the charred bodies paraded in the main city of Ahmedabad and let his own party support a state-wide strike for three days. What followed was an orgy of violence and bloodshed. Many women and young girls were raped, and many more men and women were killed. Official estimates suggest 1000 people died, but some argue it was more than 2000, mainly Muslims (Chakrabortty 2014). Modi has never acknowledged responsibility for this and points to numerous court rulings which have cleared him of any wrongdoing. However, Muslims who have family origins in the Gujarat often have a very negative view of Modi and the Bharatiya Janata Party (BJP).

Sections of the Sikh community dislike Modi for a number of reasons. It should be noted that 'Operation Bluestar', the 1984 attack on the Golden Temple, the holiest site in Sikhism, and the ensuing deadly violence by Indian government troops, was led not by the BJP but by the Congress Party, under Prime Minister Indira Gandhi. In fact, Modi has called the attack a 'dagger through India's chest' (NDTV 2014). Despite the condemnation, many associate the events with the beginnings of the growth of Indian or indeed Hindu nationalism, and so the BJP is associated in this way.

More recently, Sikhs have raised concerns that Sikh farmers who moved to Gujarat were being forcibly evicted from their land. They hold Modi personally responsible, as during his election campaign he promised Sikhs in the Punjab region of India (where the majority of Sikhs live) that these evictions would not take place (Chauhan 2014). There have been recent incidents of violence against Sikhs in both Gujarat and the Punjab, and the Sikh community, both in India and abroad, blame Modi and believe he is actively discriminating against them. They find support for this view from the fact that Explanation II of Article 25, sub-clause (b) of the Indian Constitution defines Sikhs (as well as Jains and Buddhists) as being a part of Hinduism. If they are not allowed to define their own religious identity, they argue, then the Indian government does not believe they have a right to exist. Finally, in October 2015, a copy of Guru Granth Sahib, the Sikh holy book, regarded as a living guru within Sikhism, was desecrated in a village in Punjab. Police fired on Sikhs gathering to protest, killing some and injuring others. This led to calls for Sikhs to observe a 'black Diwali', recognising that what was traditionally a time of celebration had instead become a time of mourning (Dhaliwal 2015). Sikhs in India, the UK and around the world joined in. The festival of Diwali began on 11 November 2015 and was celebrated for five days, thereby coinciding with Modi's visit to the UK. There were other sections of the Sikh community, however, who faced severe internal criticism for privately meeting with Narendra Modi during his UK visit in 2015 (Sikh24 2015).

So many Sikhs and Muslims of Indian heritage living in the UK have reason to dislike Modi, whilst many Hindus and Jains of Indian heritage support him. As noted above, different sets of coaches left Leicester to go to Wembley Stadium on 13 November 2015. Some coaches were filled with supporters, going to join in the celebrations inside the stadium. Others were filled with opponents, going to join in the protests outside. People who regularly meet and talk in Leicester at interfaith gatherings found themselves on opposite sides of an intense and emotive political divide. This story demonstrates the importance of understanding for interfaith encounter. Without knowledge of the complex political and religious background, it would be impossible to make sense of local relations between different faiths. What happens locally is impacted by actions around the world. Social media and instant messaging means people quickly receive news of what has taken place thousands of miles from them. In interfaith and other encounters I am regularly shown social media posts recording atrocities and attacks on people thousands of miles away. The actions of a police commander in the Punjab can have serious repercussions for community relations in Leicester, to give just one example.

It is not enough for an interfaith engagement to simply be about encounter. That encounter must lead to understanding of the sincerely and deeply held views. Development of understanding does not necessarily lead to agreement. Continuing the discussion of Modi's visit to the UK begun above, it is clear that Sikhs and Hindus are unlikely to come to complete agreement in their assessment of Modi, or in their religious understanding either, but they can come to a point of sincere appreciation of each other's views, a knowledge of why those views are held, and they can develop the capacity to disagree well.

The phrases 'good disagreement' and 'disagreeing well' have gained currency within the Anglican Communion, the global network of Anglican Churches, in relation to ongoing debates about human sexuality (for example, Groves 2014). The basic notion is to recognise that in some situations meaningful agreement is not possible, and rather than search for a lowest common denominator agreement, which pleases nobody and in fact dissatisfies everybody, it is preferable to develop a way of disagreeing well.

One premise of good disagreement is that appropriately managed conflict is in fact transformative and productive rather than limiting and destructive. It requires an open mind, self-reflexivity and confidence to hear one's own view challenged and another's view defended. It is difficult to achieve, but it is essential for encounter to move towards understanding, and beyond that to trust and co-operation.

Understanding is a crucial component of good disagreement, and the rest of this chapter is devoted to unpacking some of the complexities of the religious landscape in the UK to enable the reader to develop their own personal understanding, and so their ability to engage with those who think very differently from them.

Diversity within diversity

At a very superficial level, an encounter with a religious group would focus on the core elements of their beliefs. Thus, for example, when school groups first visit a mosque, they learn about the five pillars of Islam, the prescriptions of *wudu* (ritual washing), the times for prayer and so forth. However, a basic knowledge of the central tenets of Islam is insufficient for anyone who wants to truly understand Islam in the UK today. Similarly, knowing the 'Five Ks' of Sikhism is good foundational knowledge, but it is of limited value in understanding the range of views within Sikhism today.

This is not a detailed sociology of religion textbook or ethnography of the diversity of religion in the UK, and as such will not provide an exhaustive list of the diversity within religious groups in the UK today. Rather we will indicate some of the main groupings and also explain how you can work on deepening your understanding of whichever group you are particularly interested in engaging with.

Local expressions of religious diversity vary enormously and are the result of a complex mix of geographical, sociological, political, economic and religious factors. Any particular religious group will vary in how they engage with wider society, depending on the balance of these different influences.

Take Orthodox Judaism as an example. The Orthodox Jewish Community in Leicester is currently very small. So small, in fact, that they sometimes struggle to gather the *minyan*, the quorum of ten men necessary to hold a Shabbat service. This was not always the case. There is a long history of a Jewish presence in Leicester. Sir Israel Hart (1835–1911) was mayor on more than one occasion, and two more recent Jewish lord mayors were Alderman Cecil Herbert Harris (1954) and Sir Mark Henig (1967). In the 1970s the Jewish population of Leicester was around 1100, but by the 2011 Census it had dwindled to 295. The present small numbers mean the community is not very visible, and it also means that the amenities which support Orthodox Jewish life, such as shops selling food compliant with *kashrut* requirements, do not have enough of a market to be financially viable. By contrast, the Orthodox Jewish Community in Golders Green in London is far greater in number. They have the same understanding of Judaism as their fellow believers in Leicester, but the way in which they live that out in public differs, simply because of the size of the community. So even if one understands the nuances of the religious beliefs of a particular group within a given religious faith, this is not enough to enable one to understand how they are likely to behave in a particular context. A whole range of other factors must also be brought into any explanation. In what follows, a brief outline of the core beliefs of some major faiths are listed, together with some examples of diversity within diversity being outlined. This is not to provide a complete picture, but rather to indicate some trends and areas to be aware of.

Judaism

Judaism is the oldest of the Abrahamic faiths (which also include Christianity and Islam). According to the Jewish People Policy Institute, there are approximately 14.2 million Jews in the world (Associated Press in Jerusalem 2015), most of whom live in Israel and the USA, although there are Jewish minorities scattered throughout the world. Judaism traces its origins to Moses, who lived in Egypt and the surrounding region over 3500 years ago, although Jews trace their ancestry to Abraham. The Hebrew Scriptures (*tanak*) are divided into three parts. The story of the birth of Judaism is told in the *Torah*, the first five books of the Hebrew Scriptures. These are the most sacred of the books; the other two parts, the Prophets (*Nevi'im*) and Writings (*Ketuvim*), are also important but are not regarded as containing specific instructions for life as the *Torah* does.

The major groupings within Judaism are Orthodox, Reform and Progressive. The theological differences between them centre on the level of authority given to and degree of literal adherence expected of every instruction within the *Torah*. Orthodox Jews take adherence to every commandment within the *Torah* most seriously; Reform and Progressive Judaism take increasingly metaphorical and spiritual approaches to interpretation. The Jews for Jesus movement are seen as a controversial group. They identify as Jewish but also believe that the Jewish hope of a Messiah has been fulfilled in Jesus Christ. They are therefore not regarded as a Jewish group, although their worship practices are closer to Judaism than mainstream Western Christianity.

Jews are a relatively small community within the UK. The generally accepted estimate is that the population is something in the region of a quarter of a million people.[1] For the Orthodox community, in particular, the *kashrut* (dietary) laws and observance of Shabbat means they tend to congregate in particular geographical regions. Areas of Manchester, Leeds and Golders Green in London are three places with a particularly significant Jewish population but there are synagogues in most major British cities. The experience of the Holocaust (*Ha Shoah*) has left a deep and lasting scar in the consciousness of all Jews. Incidents of anti-Semitism are argued by many Jews to be indicators of intolerance within a society and there has been a steady rise in incidents. However, most Jews would accept that the UK is a haven when compared to the plight of Jews in nearby France, especially following several terrorist attacks (Freytas-Tamura 2016).

Christianity

Christians believe that God is one but three persons (Father, Son and Holy Spirit). The Son, Jesus Christ, was born to the Virgin Mary, and had a three-year itinerant ministry of preaching and miracle working before he was crucified. Christians believe that Jesus' death atoned for human failures and that Jesus did not stay dead but was resurrected and ascended to his Father in Heaven. All Christians recognise two sacraments of baptism and Holy Communion (also called the Lord's Supper or Mass). Some argue there are a further five sacraments (confession, confirmation, anointing the sick, marriage and taking holy orders). Global Christianity can be divided

---

1   The 2011 Census listed 263,346 people and this may have increased slightly.

into three main schools of thought: Orthodox, Roman Catholic and Protestant. The initial split was between the Orthodox Church, or Eastern Church, and the Roman Catholic Church, or Western Church. It occurred over a theological dispute regarding a particular clause in the creed, or confession of faith. The precise dating of the split is not completely clear but appears to have begun in the sixth century and was certainly complete by the eleventh.

In essence the debate concerns the precise nature of relationships within the Trinity and, in particular, the relationship between the Holy Spirit on the one hand and God the Father and God the Son on the other. The clause within the creed (statement of Christian belief) is often referred to by the Latin term *filioque* ('and the Son') and was included within the creed in the line referring to the Holy Spirit, so it read: 'I believe in the Holy Spirit who proceeds from the Father *and the Son* and who with the Father and the Son is worshipped and glorified.' Those who became the Orthodox Church would not accept this addition, arguing that the Holy Spirit proceeded from the Father alone and the inclusion of the *filioque* indicated a diminished understanding of God the Father. By contrast, those who became the Roman Catholic Church argued that excluding it diminished the understanding of God the Son. Neither side agreed with the other, and so there was an eventual split. To an outsider, this may seem a petty point on which to split, but it should be understood as a debate over precise understanding of who God is, hardly a trivial matter for people choosing to follow him. The Orthodox and Catholic churches have developed separately from each other and, whilst they share the overwhelming majority of core doctrinal beliefs, their practice differs somewhat. Nowadays there are significant regional variations amongst the different strands of the Orthodox Church and no one clear leader, whilst the Roman Catholic Church remains (in theory at least) united under the authority of the Pope in Rome. The Roman Catholic Church did not remain undivided after the split with the Orthodox Church. The Reformation, a schism from the Catholic Church, began in sixteenth-century Europe and gave birth to the Protestant Church. There were different nuances and geopolitical factors which influenced different countries within Europe but, in essence, the protest concerned the authority of the Pope and the inaccessibility of the Bible and church teaching, both of which were only in Latin, the language of the educated elite. Protestants were known for printing Bibles, sermons and teaching materials in the language of the ordinary people, a strategy greatly aided by the recent invention of the printing press. Birthed in protest, the Protestant Church is by no means united and has itself split into many denominations, some primarily on the basis of geography (contrast the prevalence of Lutherans in Germany with that of Anglicans in England, for example) but sometimes also on the basis of theology and practice (as for example with the growth of the Methodist Church). Protestantism includes Pentecostalism, one of the fastest-growing modern church movements. One distinct sub-group within Protestantism is the Seventh-Day Adventists, who take Saturday, not Sunday, as their holy day.

Christians debate whether groups such as Jehovah's Witnesses or the Church of Jesus Christ of Latter-Day Saints (Mormons) are indeed Christians. Most Orthodox, Catholic and Protestant Christians would say they are not, because their beliefs do not accord with orthodox teaching about the person and status of Jesus Christ. Doctrinally this is true but, from a sociological perspective, Jehovah's Witnesses and Mormons are broadly within the Christian spectrum (hence the armed forces' classification of these groups as 'Christian Tradition', as noted in Chapter 3).

Islam

Whilst many Muslims often present the Islamic community (or *ummah*) as a unified, monolithic bloc, the reality is that there are considerable variations and diversity within contemporary British Islam, let alone the global picture. The majority of Muslims in the world are Sunni but there are also Shi'a and Ibadi communities. It is estimated that 85–90 per cent of the Muslim world is Sunni, 10–15 per cent Shi'a, with very small numbers of Ibadi believers.

The Sunni, Shi'a and Ibadi differences stem from the political legacy of the Prophet Muhammad. When he died in the early seventh century, he left an Islamic nation in the Arabian Peninsula. All three traditions agree that Muhammad was the final prophet and messenger of Allah but leadership was still required. The split came from the debate over who should provide that leadership and equivocal accounts about the Prophet Muhammad's preferred choice.

The larger group of Muslims nominated Abu Bakr, a close companion and father-in-law of the Prophet, to be the next *caliph* (leader) of the Muslims and he was duly appointed. This group came to be known as Sunni. However, a smaller group believed that the Prophet's son-in-law, Ali, who was married to the Prophet Muhammad's daughter, Fatima Zahra, should become the next *caliph*. The Ibadi tradition accepts the caliphates of Abu Bakr and Umar (the second *caliph*) but take issue with aspects of the rule of Uthman (the third *caliph*) and Ali (the fourth *caliph*).

All sides point to evidence to support their views. The Prophet chose Abu Bakr to lead congregational prayers when he himself was close to death, suggesting he could be the next leader. However, Shi'as argue that Muhammad stood in front of hundreds of his companions on the way back from Hajj and claimed his family would never be led astray. They say he took Ali's hand and said that anyone who followed Muhammad should follow Ali. In essence, Shi'as follow a clan or dynastic model of succession whereas Sunnis adopt a consensual method. This division persists into our current era, with the Sunni–Shi'a divide being one underlying causal factor of some of the political violence that we witness in the Middle East today.

Both Sunni and Shi'a Islam are further sub-divided. There are four schools of jurisprudence within Sunni Islam: Hanafi, Maliki, Shafi'i and Hanbali, each named after the classical jurist who taught that particular perspective. Each school of thought tends to have particular geographical areas where it dominates but, in a country such as the UK, which includes Muslims who have origins all over the world, all four schools of thought are present. To further complicate the picture, some Sunni Muslims, rather than defining themselves by which jurisprudential school they follow, use labels such as Wahhabi, Salafi, Deobandi or Barelvi to indicate their theological position.

These distinctions are also geographical. Wahhabi Islam originated in the teaching of Muhammad ibn Abd al-Wahab in Saudi Arabia and is particularly influential in the Arab world. By contrast Deobandi Islam has its heartland in the town of Deoband in India and is particularly influential in India, Pakistan, Bangladesh and Afghanistan. There are also Sufi Muslims, who take a more spiritual approach. These are not mutually exclusive labels but potentially interconnected. So a Muslim might understand themselves to be a Sufi Barelvi, for example.

Similarly, there are different schools of thought within Shi'a Islam. The largest is the 'twelver' or Imamis, who follow the Twelfth Imam (Muhammad al Muntazar, the Awaited One), whom Shi'a Muslims believe will return at the end of time as the *al-Mahdi*, to bring peace. A smaller grouping, the Ismali, or 'sevener' Shi'a, claim allegiance to Isma'il and hence broke away at number seven, and there is another small group known as the Zaidis, who number 35–40 per cent of the population of Yemen and who disputed and broke away from the fifth Imam.

Ibadi Muslims are most prevalent in Oman and Zanzibar. They are both very conservative in a strict adherence to the Qur'an and *hadith* (sayings of the Prophet) but are also tolerant towards other faiths. Their split from the majority of Muslims is also related to the line of succession subsequent to Muhammad's death.

The position of the Ahmadiyya community within Islam is that, for the overwhelming majority, they are not classified as Muslim. Whilst Ahmadiyya Muslims share many of the beliefs of other Muslims and indeed closely accept the succession of *caliphs* followed by Sunnis, there are, however, two key theological differences. The first concerns prophets. Ahmadiyya Muslims believe that Allah still sent prophets to humanity after the death of Prophet Muhammad. They hold Muhammad in high esteem but do not regard him as the final prophet in the way Sunni and Shi'a Muslims do. For Ahmadiyyas, Mirza Ghulam Ahmad (1835–1908) was the final prophet and promised Messiah who through peaceful means would usher in the final triumph of Islam and the consummation of history. The second major difference concerns Jesus. Ahmadiyya Muslims believe Jesus is not the promised Messiah and that he survived the crucifixion. Jesus continued to preach God's message to the lost tribes of Israel until he died a natural death in Kashmir. This contrasts with Sunni Muslims, who believe that Jesus was raised to heaven and will come back to judge the world.

This very brief pen portrait is included simply to give an indication of the complexity of beliefs and structures within what is normally presented as a centralised religion. For most people engaging with Muslims, there is no need to remember all the details and nuances of the range of possible different beliefs. It is far more helpful simply to ask people what they believe and how they understand and practise Islam on a daily basis. A focus on lived, not doctrinal, religion is a more pragmatic and productive approach to take.

Hinduism

Hinduism has no known founder and hence no date of origin. It is undoubtedly the world's oldest major religious tradition. Whilst for the purposes of this brief overview we are terming it a religion, for most Hindus it is more a way of life, a rich and varied culture and world view. Hindus themselves term it *sanatana dharma*, or 'eternal law'. *Dharma*, the universal law which governs everything, includes the stratification and division of society into four *varnas* (literally 'colours', but often translated as 'castes'). These are *Brahmins*, custodians of the sacred word; *Ksatriyas*, warriors and rulers; *Vaisyas*, the backbone of society (business people, farmers, craftspeople, the middle classes); and *Sudras*, servants and labourers. Each *varna* is further subdivided, and there is also a fifth group, those of no caste, the *nihsprsya*. These are sometimes also termed *harijan*, 'God's people', and include the Dalits.

It is virtually impossible to define what is, and is not, Hinduism. It can perhaps be termed a 'family of religious beliefs', but even that definition falls short, as some identify themselves as Hindu without believing in the divine. What can be said with certainty is that the overwhelming majority of Hindus are Indian, or have Indian heritage. In recent decades, some do enter Hinduism from other backgrounds, and Nepal is notable as being the only country in the world where Hinduism is the state religion.

Most Hindus recognise two types of texts as sacred: *sruti*, that which has been revealed or perceived through hearing, as well as *smrti*, what has been remembered. *Sruti* literature is considerable, and the *smrti* literature vast; no one individual is likely to master it all. Most Hindus do not even try, but have one or two favourite texts, or even portions of texts, such as the Bhagavad Gita. Hindus traditionally hold to four stages of life, each of which has a specific aim. First, as a student, one should practise righteousness. Second, as a householder, one can focus on acquisition of material wealth and enjoyment of sensual pleasure. Third, when one's children reach adulthood, this should be renounced, as one becomes a forest dweller, leaving behind all material goods and striving for *moksha*, or final liberation. Fourth, one can focus particularly on this aim for *moksha* by becoming a 'renouncer', leaving behind all worldly goods. Hinduism understands history to be cyclical; the attainment of *moksha* is the attainment of freedom from the endless cycle of rebirth, where one's new form is determined by *karma*, the measurement of one's deeds in one's current life.

It is difficult to describe Hinduism using what are, in essence, Christian (or at least Abrahamic) theological terms. Monotheism as an Abrahamic faith construct does not have a direct equivalence within the Dharmic faiths of Hinduism and Sikhism. The differences between Hindus centre around which manifestation of deity is the central focus of worship, and four main schools of thought are commonly identified. The first, Vaishnavism, worships Vishnu and his avatars Krishna and Rama. There is a strong focus on worship in temples, and celebration of elaborate festivals, with music and singing. Second, Shaivism focuses on worship of Shiva, with an emphasis on individual asceticism and practices such as yoga. Third, Shaktism focuses on Shakti, the divine mother, who is regarded as the power who underlies the male principle. Shakti devotees often engage in *tantric* meditation. Fourth, and finally,

Smartism focuses on worshipping all the major Hindu deities. It embraces worship of all the gods and goddesses mentioned above, as well as Ganesha, Surya and Skanda. Hinduism is simultaneously a very communal and also a very individualistic faith. Each person chooses their own path of worship within the broad range of Hindu traditions, but that worship is always carried out either in community or in conscious and deliberate isolation from community, by choosing the path of a renouncer. As with the other religious traditions discussed here, there are some controversial groups. Two that are very noticeable within the UK are the Swaminarayan and ISKCON movements. Some Hindus would not recognise these groups as being Hindu, but for many in the UK they are amongst the more visible groups. The ISKCON (International Society for Krishna Consciousness, or Hare Krishna) movement is a branch of Vaishnavism, and remains both colourful and controversial. Swaminarayan Hindus worship Lord Swaminarayan, a spiritual guru who lived at the end of the eighteenth and early nineteenth centuries. Many other Hindus regard this as too modern an innovation to be an acceptable part of a religion as ancient as Hinduism.

Buddhism

Siddhartha Gautama was born in Lumbini in northern India (modern-day Nepal), in approximately 560 BCE. His father was a ruler who sheltered his son from the outside world. Despite all the attempts to isolate him, one day Gautama encountered an old man, a sick man, a dead man and a mendicant. Profoundly distressed by this encounter with suffering, Gautama chose to leave the palace and search for the answer to the problem of human pain, suffering and the meaning of life. He first tried an extremely ascetic way of life, but with little success. While he was deep in meditation under a Bodhi tree (tree of wisdom), he attained enlightenment at the age of 35. He spent the next 45 years preaching and teaching all manner of people, from the highest to the lowest. In the ensuing centuries, his teaching spread throughout Asia.

Buddha taught the four noble truths:

1. *Dukkha*: the truth that there is suffering and the reality of pain in the world.

2. *Dukkha samudaya*: the truth that suffering is caused by desire; the craving for wealth, happiness and status, which can never be satisfied, is the cause of suffering.

3. *Dukkha nirodha*: the truth that suffering will cease when people can rid themselves of all desires.

4. *Dukkha magga*: the eight-fold path as the means to escape the tyranny of desire:

    a. *Samma ditthi* (right understanding)

    b. *Samma sankappa* (right thought)

    c. *Samma vaca* (right speech)

    d. *Samma kammanta* (right action)

    e. *Samma ajiva* (right livelihood)

    f. *Samma vayama* (right effort)

    g. *Samma sati* (right mindfulness)

    h. *Samma samadhi* (right concentration).

All Buddhists subscribe to the four noble truths and the eight-fold path. But there is considerable variation in how this teaching is applied. For Theravada (School of Elders) Buddhists, the main goal is to attain *nirvana*. Similar to the Hindu concept of *moksha*, this experience of enlightenment is attained through adherence to the eight-fold path, and once attained allows one to escape from the endless cycle of birth and rebirth. Theravada Buddhism is common to Sri Lanka and Southeast Asia. Mahayana (Great Vehicle) Buddhists, on the other hand, aim to reach Buddhahood, and remain within the cycle, leading others to reach their own spiritual awakening. Mahayana Buddhism is common in East Asia, and includes sects such as Zen, Pure Land and Nichiren Buddhism. Different schools of thought within Buddhism place differing degrees of emphasis on meditation, reading of texts, ascetic practices and following Buddhist ethics.

Sikhism

The origins of Sikhism can be traced to the Punjab region of North India five centuries ago. Sikhs regard their religion as a separate entity but, from a study of religious perspective, it emerged as a reaction against contemporaneous forms of Hinduism and Islam. Sikhism (like Buddhism and Hinduism) is a Western word coined by Europeans; Sikhs use the term *Sikhi*, which comes from the Punjabi verb *sikhna*, to learn. *Sikhi* therefore indicates a disposition, a path of learning. The founder of *Sikhi*, Guru Nanak, first demonstrated this way of life through his teaching and actions, and became the model for the nine Gurus who followed him. The Sikh Gurus passed on their teachings to the community who grew around them, in the form of hymns and poems, which were enshrined in two collections: the Adi Granth and Dasam Granth. The former is normally known as Guru Granth Sahib, and is regarded not simply as a book, but as a living Guru in book form. Guru Granth Sahib is the centrepiece of any gurdwara, and integral to all Sikh worship.

All Sikhs are monotheists and engage in daily prayer and devotion to God, whom they call *Waheguru* (Wondrous Lord). Sikhism promotes the unity of God, universal love, the equality of humanity, strict moral conduct and the rejection of the caste system. The Sikh goal is to end the cycle of birth, death and reincarnation, and unite the separated individual soul with the Wondrous Lord. On attaining adulthood, a Sikh can choose to undergo initiation in the Khalsa order. This ceremony re-enacts the formation of the Khalsa order by Guru Gobind Singh. Upon completion, one becomes an *Amritdhari* (baptised) Sikh, and takes the surname *Singh* (lion) if male and *Kaur* (princess) if female. *Amritdhari* Sikhs observe the five Ks: *kesh* (hair), which should remain uncut, but cared for using a *kangha* (small wooden comb); *Amritdhari* Sikhs also wear a *kirpaan* (small sword worn to protect justice), a *kara* (iron bangle, worn to remind one to commit good deeds and that every Sikh is bound to a Guru) and *kachhera* (a special pair of undershorts). Sikhs commit to: never dishonour their hair (that is, to never cut, trim, wax, pluck or dye any bodily hair); never have an intimate relationship outside marriage; never use tobacco or other intoxicants; and never eat *kutthaa* (killed animals, so meat, fish and other related products). As with any religious tradition, Sikhs vary in how scrupulously they follow these instructions.

Sikhism is largely monolithic, although there have been two noticeable revivalist movements. The first comprises the Nirankari group, formed by Dyal Das. Responding to increased idol worship, obeisance to living gurus and the influence of Brahmanic ritual that had crept into Sikhism, he urged Sikhs to return to their focus on *nirankar* (the formless divine). They remain a fringe sect with only a small following. The other group are the Namdharis, founded by Baba Ram Singh in the 1850s. They had a greater impact, due to their focus on Khalsa identity and the authority of Guru Granth Sahib. One of their idiosyncrasies was the loud and almost frenzied repetition of *nam*, which culminates in a frenzied howling or shrieking *kuk* of the name. Ram Singh was given the status of a living Guru by his followers, a belief that is heterodox to most Sikhs. Many of Ram Singh's followers believed in an apocryphal text, the *sau sakhi*, which foretold a decline in foreign rule and a return to Sikh rule. This teaching meant Namdhari Sikhs were regarded with suspicion by the British, and their leader Ram Singh was interned when he issued a circular urging his followers to congregate in Amritsar in 1857. Despite being imprisoned, his following had grown to over 100,000 by the 1860s. Namdhari Sikhs remain a small minority within the Sikh diaspora. Greater differentiation will exist in terms of how seriously individuals take the five Ks and the *Sikhi* rule of life and also in political views in relation to the desire for a Sikh homeland of Khalistan (an aspiration which essentially means the creation of an independent country from Punjab in India and Sikh-dominated areas of neighbouring Indian states and also Pakistan).

How to best respond?

The main aim of this chapter has been to make clear the incredible diversity and variation there is within every religion. There is something in human nature that means we do not remain united in practising our faith, whatever it may be. Rather than make the discussion overly exhaustive (and potentially exhausting), we have only given brief overviews of six of the major religions. A discussion of Paganism would have revealed the many nuances and varieties present within polytheistic nature worship, including Wicca, Witchcraft, Druidry, Heathenry, Shamanism and Hellenism. An investigation of Jainism would have noted the main split into *Svetambaras* and *Digambaras* and also further sub-divisions within this binary. This could have continued for other faiths, although it should be noted that smaller groups (such as the Baha'i) tend to be more unified. Even those who do not believe in any deity at all are not a unified group, with varying degrees of agnosticism and atheism and debates about appropriate humanist practices illustrating the point.

The chapter has modelled the best approach to understanding this diversity, which is to treat each religion on its own terms, and engage with the individual belief of the person with whom you are engaging. This is not to say you need to assume all beliefs are equally valid or equally true. Rather, in order to understand, one must take belief seriously; we live in a society which claims to give equal space to everyone to believe what they want, so long as it does not harm others. The only way to model that is for us to take seriously what other people believe, to try and see the world from their perspective and to understand what challenges this world view brings.

Where to find out more?

This chapter has only given the briefest outline of some aspects of major world faiths. There is a lot more that you could read if you want to find out more. The internet includes many useful resources.[2] Short guides, such as the Oxford University Press *A Very Short Introduction* series or the Oneworld *Beginners' Guides* or the *Teach Yourself* series, all have accessible, easy-to-read introductions to major world faiths. The St Philip's Centre principle is that it is good to read, but it is even more important to talk with people. Religion is taught but also lived, and you

---

2   Including sites such as www.bbc.co.uk/religion or www.interfaith.org.uk.

can only really capture lived experience through talking with people.

CASE STUDY 4.1: WORK UNIFORMS

Individuals and organisations looking for advice in relation to a wide variety of issues periodically approach the St Philip's Centre. One recent example concerned work uniforms. An individual approached the Centre on behalf of their employing organisation to discuss issues related to religious attire and appropriate clothing for cleaning staff. At the heart of the matter was a conflict between two imperatives: a religiously motivated imperative to wear certain types of clothing and a health and safety motivated imperative to ensure employees were able to perform their duties safely. The particular concern was whether a particular Islamic dress code, of long flowing skirts, was compatible with performing duties as a cleaner.

The St Philip's Centre does not give advice on what can and cannot be legally enforced in terms of work uniform, since we are not professionally qualified to do so. Hence what follows is not a legal opinion. But we are able to help people understand the range of viewpoints within a given religious tradition. In this case, we noted that not every Muslim would interpret the Qur'anic injunction towards modesty to necessarily demand that women wore skirts which went below their ankles. This enabled the employer to recognise that some other Muslim women, who also worked as cleaners for the same organisation, actually wore quite short skirts. Moreover, we were able to open up the question to the variety of perspectives that are inevitably brought to bear. Whilst many Sikh or Hindu women might not choose to wear the standard cleaner's uniform of shapeless trousers and polo shirt, they recognise that these are the clothes their employer gives them to perform their duties and dress in accordance with the employer's wishes.

The question of what religious clothing and identification is compatible with wearing a work uniform has a significant history, and there have been a number of high-profile cases. A more historic example would concern the right of Sikhs to wear a turban. A more recent one concerns the right of Christian Nadia Eweida to wear a cross visibly over her British Airways uniform (BBC 2013a). What is striking about this case is that while Ms Eweida won her case, in the same ruling the European Court of Human Rights dismissed a case brought by a nurse, Shirley Chaplin, whose employer had also stopped her wearing a necklace with a cross. This suggests that the practical demands of working in particular environments bring different levels of permission to display religious affiliation in public. In a food preparation area of a large commercial food business, for example, no jewellery could be worn, with the possible exception of a wedding ring (and that is simply because many people find their wedding ring impossible to remove).

The Islamic full face covering, or *niqab*, is particularly controversial in relation to work uniforms. The *niqab* has been subject to high-profile disagreement for some time in the United Kingdom, with former Labour Home Secretary Jack Straw declaring in 2006 that he felt uncomfortable talking with a woman whose face was covered (Straw 2006). In 2016 the topic became more controversial when suggestions were made that it might be appropriate for a serving police officer to wear a full face veil while on active duty. The Chief Constable of West Midlands Police, David Thompson, said it would be acceptable, and other forces have indicated they would at least consider any request if it were made. This may, in part, be a reflection of a desire to increase the diversity of the police workforce, although media coverage of the idea was largely negative, arguing that members of the public would not feel comfortable reporting a crime to a person whose face they could not see (Dean 2016; Warzynski 2016). What is striking about this debate is that whilst Leicestershire Police issued a relatively bland statement saying they would consider a request for full face covering if it were made, which was then clarified further with a second statement that no such request had been made to date, national newspapers sensationalised the possibility, suggesting burka-clad police officers were an imminent possibility. The reality is that this is unlikely to ever happen. Louise Casey's report (Casey 2016) was very critical of the police in this regard.

Employers have the right, within reason, to dictate what their employees wear. People have the right to choose to not work for an employer who might make them wear something they would rather not. Somewhere within these two rights an appropriate balance must be sought.

5

TRUST

TOM WILSON

Many English primary schools have a daily act of 'collective worship', more commonly referred to as an assembly. As a member of the clergy, I have often taken these, and I do my best to challenge the children to think carefully about an issue that is relevant to their lives. When it came to talking about trust, I decided the only way for them to learn what trust is would be for me to model it and for them to experience it. So, at the start of the assembly, I took out my wallet, and removed the five £20 notes that were inside. I explained I had mistakenly brought too much money with me to school and asked for a pupil to volunteer to look after it. Once I had selected my volunteer from the forest of hands which went up, I gave her the money and asked her to count it. There was some surprise at the idea of giving a pupil £100 to look after. But it started some of them thinking. That pupil sat on one side, while we continued thinking about trust as a group, using some of the classic trust game exercises, such as walking blindfolded past obstacles whilst someone else guides you, and falling backwards, while trusting that someone else will catch you. At the end of the assembly, I reminded the pupils about the money, and asked for it back. The pupil handed it over, and they all left that hall. When nearly all of them were gone,

I went to put the money back into my wallet. Without really thinking I counted it as I returned it. An eagle-eyed teacher spotted me and commented quietly to me as he left, 'If you really trusted her, you wouldn't have had to count the money, would you?'

He was right. If we really trust someone, we have no need to check up on them, no need to scrutinise what they are doing. Trust is a very strong virtue, which is difficult to obtain, but very easy to lose. When the staff and trustees of the St Philip's Centre were deciding on the values which define us, we rejected tolerance, respect and honour as possible options for this third value. Whilst they may be good in and of themselves, each of these are limited virtues, in a way that trust is not.

Do more than just tolerate, respect or honour

Tolerance, as I would define it, is a very limited virtue. An individual can be tolerated but at the same time ignored. Furthermore, and more crucially, tolerance assumes an imbalance of power, as power-holders tolerate those weaker than them. Thus Tariq Ramadan describes tolerance as 'intellectual charity on the part of the powerful' (2010, p.47). In his view, tolerance is not something to welcome, because it is of a very limited nature. He argues that we tolerate without accepting, without liking or caring for the other person. Tolerance is therefore understood as a condescending welcome of a weaker person, a conditional acceptance that perpetuates that weakened status. Luke Bretherton suggests there are three conditions necessary for tolerance. First, conduct about which one disapproves, even if only mildly. Second, the disapprover(s), who have the power to act coercively against or interfere with that of which they disapprove but chose not to. Third, the lack of interference must result from more than acquiescence, indifference or a balance of power. Thus Bretherton argues that tolerance is effectively the powerful not wanting something to happen but choosing to let it happen anyway (2010, pp.122–6).

It is important to notice the power dynamic that both Tariq Ramadan and Luke Bretherton identify. They are both sceptical about tolerance precisely because it perpetuates an imbalance of power. If I stick to merely tolerating you, then I remain in a position of power over you. You remain weak, whilst I remain strong. A question to consider is whether I accept tolerance as a positive step because it allows me to maintain my position of power and not have my situation disrupted in any way. If I think tolerance is sufficient, is it because this allows me to maintain my power?

Although tolerance is a limited virtue, it does have a role to play. Take, for example, the 1689 British Parliament Act of Toleration, which allowed Non-conformist Christians freedom of worship. The Act was a positive first step, a way of limiting or eliminating conflict, especially conflict within the Christian world. Tolerance is to be welcomed as an initial action, a move beyond hatred, but it is no more than that. It is not a peak to ascend, but a foothill from which to climb towards peaceful co-operation and mutual self-understanding. In some situations, it can be a massive challenge to get to a point where all sides in a conflict recognise that everyone else has a right to exist. To pick one international example, if all sides in the Israel/Palestine conflict were able to agree that everyone involved had a right to exist, then this would be a cause for some celebration. In these circumstances, a grudging tolerance of an enemy would be a very positive step.

Moreover, not everyone understands tolerance negatively. For some people, words such as tolerance and respect are entirely interchangeable. A school inclusion manager once explained to me the very positive ethos of her Anglican school as being characterised by 'the tolerance of other religions, a recognition, a strong value put on faith, and tolerance and mutual understanding, and the importance of faith'. For her, tolerance was an entirely positive virtue, with none of the negative connotations outlined above. She was, of course, a person of power within the school hierarchy, and so perhaps not the best placed to explore the nuances between tolerance, respect, honour and trust.

Some people argue in favour of respect as a virtue to promote in place of tolerance, but does respect go far enough? It is not that respect is a bad thing; the question is whether something more is needed. Respect does not necessarily take relationships much deeper than tolerance. The power dynamic is still uneven; there is still no need for close engagement. Respect can remain distant, an arm's-length virtue. The same is true for honour. We can honour someone without necessarily engaging with them. I have written elsewhere about the types of friendships Christians can develop with Muslims, and the same metaphor can be extended to all types of relationship-crossing boundaries (Wilson 2015). For real co-operation to take place, trust is the necessary virtue.

Beginning with trust

Sometimes engagement should start with establishing trust. The St Philip's Centre runs an annual encounter programme for a three-year degree course training Christian youth workers. The programme lasts two days and is part of the second-year students' module on diversity awareness. It focuses almost entirely on visits to places of worship and face-to-face encounters with people of faiths other than Christianity. For many of the participants this is their first serious engagement with people who have a sincere religious faith that is not Christianity. Some participants are understandably nervous about the programme, feeling unsure about what they will be asked to do and in particular whether they will be expected to take part in worship which they would consider to be idolatry. For some Christians concerned to be loyal to Jesus Christ above all else, the idea of being asked to make an offering to a Hindu *murti*, or to bow to the Sikh holy scriptures (Guru Granth Sahib Ji), is a deeply unsettling notion. It is important, therefore, that the course organisers establish appropriate bonds of trust at the start of the programme, offering reassurance that participants will be asked to observe, and not participate in, worship.

Even this reassurance was not sufficient for one participant. His primary concern was his allegiance to Jesus Christ and, in his view, even entering another place of worship was unacceptable. In order to complete his degree, he had to participate in some form of engagement with someone of another faith, but he flatly refused to come on the programme organised by the St Philip's Centre. In the end a compromise was reached, whereby he visited a Muslim imam in his own home, interviewing him and talking about how he saw his role within the Muslim community. Trust had to be established for this to take place. Trust that the imam was a safe person to meet with, trust that nothing untoward would take place and trust that it was acceptable for a Christian to behave in this way. Paradoxically, this individual's refusal to participate in the standard programme actually led to a deeper one-to-one encounter, which arguably resulted in increased understanding. It is unlikely that he moved to a point of heart-to-heart trust but he did move beyond tolerance at a distance, and any progress must be celebrated as progress.

This example has utilised a trainee Christian youth worker, but the need to begin with trust does not rest exclusively with Christians. Theologically conservative members of any faith tradition often need reassuring about the nature of any encounter before they are willing to participate in it. Some Muslim parents have concerns about their children visiting churches and other places of worship as part of their RE lessons and need to be reassured that worship will not take place. Sometimes even the children themselves share those concerns (although at other times, they are eager to go, if only as a means of rebelling against their parents). Some Hindus and Sikhs will not engage in interfaith encounter with Christians because of concerns that the real Christian agenda is about conversion. As with the example above, trust is the necessary prerequisite for meaningful encounter to take place.

At the heart of any concerns about interfaith encounter are issues of power and authority. Those who lack trust in the meeting are invariably the ones with less power in that particular context. Their lack of trust is rooted in a concern that the more powerful will abuse their power to enforce their own perspective on others. When faced with this situation it is important to work hard at establishing trust by demonstrating, through word and action, an awareness of the power dynamics and a commitment to use power appropriately. We may not be able to completely level the playing field, as some power is inherent in particular roles, but we can at least demonstrate self-awareness and a desire to mitigate against any imbalance of power.

So how do you establish trust? The first step is to recognise that trust is lacking. This can be done in a number of ways. A simple exercise at the start of a programme can be to ask people to form a 'human rainbow', indicating their position in a continuum of opinions from 'I am really looking forward to this encounter' to 'I am really dreading this encounter'. This can be done silently, to simply acknowledge the range of feelings in the room or, if time allows and it is appropriate, people from across the spectrum of opinions can be invited to share their thoughts. These must be received without judgement; there are no right or wrong feelings before encounter takes place. What is important is to acknowledge what is, to recognise the reality of people's feelings and enable them to decide how they are going to deal with them.

It is also helpful for course leaders to explain the nature of the programme and in particular to distinguish between appropriate respect (removing shoes and covering your head when entering a gurdwara, for example) and participating in worship. For some learners, participation is important, and so receiving *Prasad* from a gurdwara or mandir helps them fully engage with the lived religious experience of those whom they are visiting. For others, this is an uncomfortable experience, which they would rather avoid. Explaining that participation is optional and that individuals can make their own choices is crucial for establishing and maintaining trust.

Ultimately trust rests on the honesty, integrity and transparency of those running the programme and the hosts in the places of worship visited. It is therefore crucial to work hard at keeping lines of communication open and active, especially when establishing ongoing working relationships with particular faith communities.

CASE STUDY 5.1: THE PREVENT STRATEGY

One area of the St Philip's Centre's work where trust is essential is our work related to the Prevent strategy, which is part of the UK government's counter-terrorism strategy. Prevent is one of the four Ps of the wider Contest strategy, the other three being Prepare, Pursue and Protect. The overall aim of Prevent is, as the name suggests, 'to reduce the threat to the UK from terrorism by stopping people becoming terrorists or supporting terrorism' (HM Government 2015a, p.5). On one level, it is difficult to argue with this – the overwhelming majority of people are not in favour of terrorism motivated by any persuasion or of people becoming terrorists. The difficulty comes in how that aim is realised in real life.

The Contest strategy began in 2003 and has been through a number of adjustments due to governmental and ministerial changes. However, the broad thrust of the strategy has remained whether a Labour, Conservative–Liberal coalition or Conservative government has been in power. One recent revision was in 2015 with the onset of the public sector Prevent duty which mandated organisations to give due regard to the aims of Prevent. No government strategy is without its context, and the context of Prevent is that it has a very negative reputation within sections of the media and many Muslim community organisations. It is perceived as being heavy-handed and ill-informed; an excuse to introduce the surveillance state to control and reform Islam. It is blamed for criminalising Muslims (Mohammed 2015) and introducing an overly muscular liberalism (O'Toole 2015). Moreover, a former senior police official, Dal Babu, is also on record questioning the effectiveness of the current Prevent strategy (Halliday and Dodd 2015). Indeed, confidence is so low for one individual, Dr Salmann Butt, that he has taken the government to court, arguing that Prevent is an infringement of his human rights (BBC 2016d).

In 2011 the St Philip's Centre agreed to employ Leicestershire's Prevent Co-ordinator. We were invited to do so by Leicester City Council and did so in consultation with the Federation of Muslim Organisations (FMO), who at the time were the local authority's main infrastructure body for the Muslim community. The Prevent Co-ordinator is tasked with overseeing the delivery of the Prevent strategy within Leicester, Leicestershire and Rutland. We believe that, although legitimate questions can be raised about the detail of the implementation of the Prevent strategy, it is preferable for the St Philip's Centre to be actively engaged in shaping the delivery of Prevent on the ground than to not be involved at all. Equally, if we are to be an interfaith organisation with nous, then ignoring or removing oneself from the debates associated with Prevent would weaken our profile. Hence, we have continued to employ the Prevent Co-ordinator until the time of writing, December 2016.

What are the particular concerns?

A number of stories are regularly used to illustrate concerns around the Prevent strategy, of which three merit particular attention. These are the 'terrorist house' story; the 'eco-terrorist' story; and the 'cucumber story'. Each illustrates the challenge of establishing appropriate bonds of trust. Advocates of Prevent argue that each story presents misinformation about the strategy, whilst opponents argue they are indicative of the flawed nature of the strategy as a whole.

The 'terrorist house' story is taken as a sign of the disproportionate nature of the Prevent duty, which is part of the Counter-Terrorism and Security Act 2015 and means educational and health establishments have a statutory duty to report any concerns they have that an individual they have contact with may be in danger of committing a violent extremist act (HM Government 2015b). The 'terrorist house' story is that police visited a ten-year-old boy, who lives in Accrington in Lancashire, at home after he wrote that he lived in a 'terrorist house' in a school lesson. Apparently, this was a simple spelling mistake, and he meant to say he lived in a 'terraced house' (BBC 2016e). Critics take this as an example of the heavy-handed application of the Prevent duty in schools, suggesting that innocent mistakes are routinely treated as major security threats and otherwise peaceful people are targeted as though they are criminals. When critics of the Prevent strategy retell this story, they rarely mention that the boy was not in fact questioned by anti-terrorist police but by community-based officers in conjunction with social services. Nor do they discuss the fact that the police were in fact acting in response to concerns being raised by the school about the boy's safety and wellbeing (Gani and Slawson 2016), since the first line in the work which included the 'terrorist house' comment was 'I hate it when my uncle hits me' (Withnall 2016). Thus a story that is told about Prevent is not actually about Prevent, despite what popular misconceptions suggest.

The 'eco-terrorist' story concerns a 14-year-old boy, who used the word 'l'ecoterrorisme' in a French lesson while discussing environmental activism. He is a Muslim and was subsequently questioned by school authorities who wanted to establish whether he had any links with so-called Islamic State or supported Islamist terrorism in any way (Dodd 2015). Whilst the school may have been over-zealous in acting on their concerns, no further action was taken, the incident has never been a Prevent referral and an attempt to initiate a judicial review alleging religious discrimination was thrown out of court (Casey 2016, p.155).

The 'cucumber' story refers to a four-year-old boy in Luton, who when asked to explain a drawing of his father cutting a cucumber described it as a 'cucker-bum', which staff heard as a 'cooker bomb' and concluded he was talking about his father making improvised explosive devices (Quinn 2016). As with the 'eco-terrorist' case mentioned above, staff at the boy's nursery did initially raise concerns but, when they contacted the authorities, they advised the nursery staff that no further action needed to be taken.

These are three of the main stories which those who oppose Prevent regularly use to argue that the whole strategy is flawed. They have gained some traction in popular consciousness, and hence make the task of establishing trust with communities difficult, a point noted by Chief Constable Simon Cole QPM, National Police Chiefs Lead on the Prevent strategy, in a comment piece for the *Guardian* newspaper (Cole 2016). The St Philip's Centre recognises that people do have a wide variety of concerns both about government policy and also police behaviour as a whole, which are normally focused exclusively on Prevent, as this is well known to the general public. In essence, concerns centre on two areas: freedom of speech, and profiling of Muslims as presenting a particular threat.

The issue of freedom of speech is especially pertinent in educational settings. All those involved in education, whether at a primary, secondary or tertiary level, agree that the freedom to explore ideas and experiment with concepts and points of view is essential to a rounded education. This necessarily includes discussion of extremist or divisive ideas. For some people, the 'eco-terrorist' story is taken as symptomatic of a concerted drive by government to curtail freedom of expression.

So, the argument advanced by opponents of Prevent is that those engaged with implementing the Prevent strategy are using it to curtail freedom of expression. However, those who work on the strategy argue that they are in favour of freedom of speech, provided that this freedom is consistent and not abused to promote hatred of, or violence towards, any individual or group. The problem comes with implementation of the detail of the strategy. Whilst those who are familiar with the issues have a robust understanding of what constitutes acceptable speech and what does not, there are many people who work in institutions that have a statutory duty to 'have due regard for the aims of' Prevent but are poorly trained or lack the confidence to make complex and challenging decisions. For there to be greater trust, there needs to be a greater understanding of the complexity of the issues and the process by which decisions are made. So, if anything, there is a need for more resources to be included in this area, to enable more in-depth training for all those who have a statutory duty to engage with these issues.

The second main concern is around who is targeted by the Prevent strategy. This is a particularly sensitive area. Whilst it is only a very small minority in any community who resort to violence, nevertheless there are a number of people who self-identify as Muslim who are attracted to violent acts in the name of Islam. It is not for us to determine whether someone is, or is not, a Muslim, or whether particular actions are, or are not, Islamic. Every religious tradition has the potential to be subverted to violent ends. If we take a global and a chronological view, we can soon see that many religions have been used in this way at some time. There are reports of incidents of violence by Hindus against Muslims, Christians and Sikhs in India (Staufenburg 2016), of Buddhists attacking Muslims in Burma (IRIN 2016) and Christians attacking Muslims in the Central African Republic (IRIN 2014), to give just three examples. Religion can always be subverted and used as a rationale for violence. That is not to say every religious person or community is violent. But religious faith does not preclude violence and has the potential to be subverted in the cause of violence.

In the United Kingdom in the early twenty-first century, one of the main threats of terrorism, according to the security services, comes from those who identify themselves as Muslims. In an interview, Andrew Parker, the head of MI5, listed three threats: Islamic-inspired terror, terrorism in Northern Ireland and covert action by foreign states. He added that 'My expectation is that we will find and stop most attempts at terrorism in the country', noting that his use of the caveat 'most' indicated that since the current threat level in the UK is 'severe' this meant 'there will be terrorist attacks in this country' (Johnson and MacAskill 2016). There is also a substantial reciprocal threat from those motivated by neo-Nazi and far right ideologies. The Prevent strategy also works in tackling this threat, providing support and challenge where needed to disrupt those motivated towards violence from a far right ideology (Baldet 2016). Since a small minority within far right and Muslim groups present the main threat, it is only logical that security services are particularly focused on these two groups. However, recognition of the general area of threat does not mean any Muslim, or anyone who expresses far right views, is necessarily a threat. Those involved in Prevent work fully understand that being religiously conservative is not the same as being an extremist or indeed a violent extremist. The picture is a very complex one and, without acknowledging that complexity, trust cannot be established.

We establish trust with those whom we work with by hearing their concerns, addressing them as far as we are able to and also by talking about the nature of the threat which the Prevent strategy is trying to tackle.

What is the threat?

The Prevent strategy is one of a number of ways in which the UK government confronts violent extremism, but how do people become dangerous extremists? There are two aspects to this discussion. The first is a practical one: are there particular spaces or causal factors that should be noted? The second is more dispositional: are certain types of people more likely to be attracted? These two are closely connected but, in order to develop a logical progression of argument, we will begin with a brief discussion of online recruitment as an example of a particular space before commenting on two studies that suggest particular types of individuals may be more susceptible to recruitment.

The online space is a particularly contested one and impossible to control. The government is very well aware of the challenge of providing a positive narrative of life in the UK in the internet world. The counter-extremism strategy states their intention to 'continue to confront and challenge extremist propaganda, ensuring no space goes uncontested, including online, promoting a better alternative, and supporting those at risk of radicalisation' (HM Government 2015a, p.17). The internet is a fertile recruiting ground for both Islamic and neo-Nazi/far right extremists. Berger (2015) discusses Daesh's (to use the Arabic description for so-called Islamic State) online recruiting strategy in some detail. He argues that there are at the time of his writing (October 2015) around 40,000 Twitter accounts actively supporting Daesh, of which around 2000 are active in English. There are numerous other social media outlets and message platforms where Daesh is also active, indicating that the true scale of the challenge is considerable. A more recent report by Daniel Milton (2016) noted that the peak of Daesh media output came in August 2015, but that they still produced 196 media outputs in August 2016.

Berger outlines the process that Daesh recruiters use. First contact may be made either by the recruit or recruiters, who engage with both radical and mainstream online Islamic networks. Once that contact has been made, a small community quickly surrounds the target, interacting with them in high-volume bursts. Some may publish 50 or 60 tweets per day, 'with some prolific users clocking over 250 on given days'. During this phase, Daesh supporters encourage the target to isolate from those who do not support Daesh. This will include other Muslims. This creates a much stronger relationship between the recruiter(s) and the target and enables them to encourage the target to shift to more private communication channels, whether the private messaging function on Twitter or an encrypted messaging application such as WhatsApp, Kik, Surespot and Telegram. During this more private discussion, the recruiter then determines what course of action the target is most likely to take and encourages steps in that direction. Some individuals may be more likely to commit acts of terror in their own country, while others may be open to the possibility of travelling overseas, but both could potentially be of benefit to Daesh. Milton analysed 9000 Daesh media outputs in the period January 2015 to August 2016. He concluded that 48 per cent related to military issues, 20 per cent to governance of Daesh-controlled territory, 7 per cent to commercial, 7 per cent to religious matters and 19 per cent to other issues. Thus more than half of the Daesh media output in the period analysed was not related to military issues at all, and therefore violence is not the sole, or indeed main, recruiting tool used (Milton 2016, p.30).

In a briefing paper prepared for the Institute for Strategic Dialogue, Ramalingam states that the far right 'frequently communicate and operate through social media, semi-public and password-protected forums'. He adds that the potential of social media for recruitment, mobilisation and propaganda is exploited to bring a sense of comradeship and ownership of the far right movement. Ramalingam adds that a noticeable trend amongst extreme far right use of the internet has been the focus on youth, 'reflecting a youth lifestyle and employing recognisable styles, slogans and symbols'. He adds that the internet has 'vastly expanded the market niche and profitability of White Power music and has made it an important source of international income for extreme right movements' (Ramalingam 2014, pp.14–15).

There are many benefits to social media and the online space. We are not seeking to demonise technology but simply to point out the game-changing nature of online recruitment. Face-to-face engagement can potentially be a fertile source of recruits for dangerous extremists and it is noticeable that prisons, for example, have been cited in these terms. However, the pervasive reach of the internet means that a 12-year-old boy fiddling unsupervised on his tablet in his bedroom may unwittingly stumble across a Daesh recruiter and be led down a path towards violent action or emigration to Syria before anyone realises what is happening.

This brings us to the second point: who might be in particular danger of becoming radicalised? Jennifer Kavanagh discusses the impact of poverty on terrorist group participation. A general view might be that poverty would increase the likelihood of participation in a terrorist group, because poverty may lead to desperation manifesting itself in violent action. Kavanagh does not find this general thesis necessarily persuasive. She suggests that it is only when experience of poverty is combined with at least a high school education that likelihood of participation in a terrorist organisation increases. She supports her hypothesis with analysis of data related to membership of Hezbollah (Kavanagh 2011).

Kavanagh's argument is therefore that failed expectation is a crucial factor in increasing susceptibility to terrorist recruitment. In his study of young Muslim men in London and Madrid, Justin Gest (2010) similarly argues that individual experiences of political expectations being fulfilled is the key determinant for whether an individual engages with political systems. Gest's main point is that the failure to meet expectations, *whether those expectations were reasonable or not*, is the main reason for individuals becoming isolated, alienated, apart and likely to engage in what he calls 'anti-system' behaviour. Similarly, Louise Richardson (2006, pp.71–103) argues that terrorists are primarily motivated by what she terms the 'Three Rs': revenge, renown and reaction. Terrorists seek revenge against an oppressor for acts of violence already committed against them; try to establish renown for themselves and the cause they represent; and act in a way that seeks to provoke a reaction, especially a reaction of fear which is disproportionate to the actual threat posed. Likewise, Kamaldeep Bhul argues, on the basis of a small pilot study, that those who are more sympathetic to terrorism or violent protest tend to be more socially isolated, but they are not poor and did not report more discrimination than those who condemned or were neutral about terrorism and violent protest. Those who were more sympathetic to violence were also less politically engaged and had more depressive symptoms in the two-week period before the survey, although he is clear that there is no direct causal link between mental health concerns and sympathy for terrorist action (Conversation 2016).

What to do about Prevent?

The brief overview of research into the area of who becomes a dangerous extremist suggests that educated but financially disadvantaged and socially isolated young people with access to a smartphone are potentially amongst the most likely to become dangerous extremists. In concluding his discussion about Daesh online recruitment, Berger notes:

> The majority of those who post messages in support of the Islamic State on social media will never act out. There is no consensus on when radical rhetoric signals a move to violence, at what point intervention is appropriate, or what type of intervention is most appropriate. (2015, p.23)

This is another part of the complexity. When does espousing extremist views move into extremist action? This is not necessarily a linear process; there is no single conveyor belt to radicalisation. Grindrod and Sloggett (2010) suggest that an analogy with the board game snakes and ladders is more appropriate. They describe the ladders as points where individuals make a greater commitment to their cause, and the snakes are moral hazards that prohibit commitment to the cause, of which the Prevent strategy is one small part. Even this analogy is limited, as it still includes a linear process. Be that as it may, some people may choose at some point in time to take violent action. This is the potential threat that the Prevent strategy is trying to meet. In October 2016 the Metropolitan Police's head of counter-terrorism, Neil Basu, noted that counter-terrorism and security services had foiled at least ten attacks in the past two years, and have around 550 live investigations at any one time. He stated that Prevent is an important element of the strategy to respond to this threat (National Police Chiefs' Council (NPCC) 2016).

The particular challenge for Prevent is that it operates in the so-called 'pre-criminal' space. That is to say, it seeks to prevent individual(s) engaging in criminal activity. Therefore, its success is primarily in things not happening, in attacks not taking place. The police calculate that between April 2007 and 31 March 2014 there were 3934 referrals to the Channel programme (NPCC 2014).

Channel is described as 'a multi-agency approach to identify and provide support to individuals who are at risk of being drawn into terrorism' (HM Government 2015c, p.3). It is a voluntary process in which professionals from different sectors, including health, social care, education, the police and community stakeholders, meet together to devise a programme of support to work with an individual viewed as vulnerable to being drawn towards terrorism or extremism.

However, many measurable success stories are hesitantly publicised, if at all. Part of this is about preventing 'copycat' incidents, and another aspect is, if the criminal actions were part of a broader network, to ensure that that closing off of one avenue does not jeopardise further investigations.

Although publicity is rare, recently *The Times* ran an article that gave some details about Channel (Rumbelow 2016). Helen Rumbelow describes the case of a boy whom she calls Ali (not his real name). He drew a picture of a gun being fired in a detention, which in and of itself is not an especially threatening action. But when his teacher tried to talk with him about the drawing, 'Ali hunched, avoided eye contact and gnawed at the skin of his fingers, making them bloody and raw.' He explained that he wanted to fight for Islamic State. Ali's mother, Yasmeen, was invited to the school, shown the drawing and asked if she would like to refer her son to Channel, which she agreed to do. His personal circumstances were challenging: an abusive father, from whom the whole family had fled, as well as bullying at school. Ali's anger at his own life experience led him to watching violent videos online, where he confused the Pakistani Army and so-called Islamic State. The Channel programme arranged a series of interventions: a GP prescribed treatment for Ali's hand biting; a social worker isolated the bully at school and helped Ali develop his self-confidence; a youth worker expanded his social life; Yasmeen led discussions about the family's future; and the imam from a moderate, liberal mosque met one-to-one with Ali several times. Ali's access to the internet is now quite restricted and monitored by his mother. He was transformed by the intervention, and Rumbelow was clearly impressed by what she had seen, stating: 'I find myself amazed that our public services actually work this well in concert. It is as though they have woven the fabric of civil society around this boy.' This is the type of work that Channel is engaged in; complex but transformative when done right.

The strategy adopted by the St Philip's Centre is to invite people to enter into the complexity, to help them see the dilemmas for themselves and to suggest their own solutions. At the heart of this strategy is an understanding that rather than taking power over individuals or groups, we must share power with them and empower them to tackle the problems they face. Although we are all at risk, it is the Muslim community which faces a particular threat from terrorism in the name of Islam, and it is disadvantaged and deprived white majority communities who face a particular threat from far right and neo-Nazi extremism. Therefore, they must be the communities who are given the greatest power to tackle the issues. Hence an important part of our strategy is to have a community reference group, who meet quarterly to discuss Prevent work and offer constructive and critical feedback as to how we are carrying it out. We do, however, note one particular challenge, namely that whilst civil society in the Muslim community is active, the same is not true in some other communities. There are reference points to call upon to access Muslim views, but where and who are the mainstream voices for the white majority population? And in particular, how can we best engage those with extreme right-wing views?

How to establish trust?

There are a number of basic steps that must be taken if trust is to be established. The most crucial concerns attitude. If the organisers of any inter- or intrafaith encounter choose to trust, then this will communicate to all participants. Organisers must also choose to sit lightly to the power they have, allowing other people appropriate control over what takes place. For any programme to run smoothly, there must be a degree of structure and organisation, but this does not have to be done in a domineering fashion.

If a long-term process of engagement is envisaged, then it is essential to begin with clear boundaries and expectations of the engagement for everyone to be honest about what they are hoping for and realistic about what might be achieved. These expectations should be recorded and revisited regularly throughout the engagement, to ensure everyone still agrees and is still on board with them.

Practical details are also crucial. Take food as an example. A strict Jain diet is not only fully vegetarian (no meat or fish, or any related products) but also vegan, ruling out eggs, and moreover avoiding onions and garlic. For a Jain to genuinely participate in any encounter where food is involved, they would need reassurance that their dietary needs are catered for. This is, of course, true for anyone who has dietary needs, whether religious, medical or simply personal preference. Organisers must therefore make sure they check the details of what is required and not make an issue of meeting those needs. This is not always as straightforward as may be supposed, as whilst some people will insist on strictly vegan food, others will object if they are not served meat. Developing appropriate ways of balancing conflicting demands is crucial.

There are also many different cultural expectations regarding the position of a leader, such as who gets to talk, for how long and in what order they should speak. At least some consideration, certainly more than simple lip service, should be paid to those concerns, unless there are very valid reasons why this is not possible.

Trust is primarily generated over time. If I consistently demonstrate my awareness of power dynamics, my concern for your wellbeing and my willingness to work for your good, even if it costs me, then trust can be earned. The story that Jesus told of a man who is mugged and is then ignored by two individuals but helped by a third is one of the better known in the Bible. It occurs in Luke 10.25–37, and is traditionally termed the parable of the Good Samaritan. The story is told in response to a question about 'who is my neighbour?' and recounts how a man is mugged and left for dead. The first two people who pass him, a

Jewish priest and a Levite, pass by and ignore him, but the third, a Samaritan, cares for him. This was somewhat surprising, since Jews and Samaritans were sworn enemies. The story is taken as teaching about how we can care for those who are different from ourselves and is sometimes used by Christians for critical self-reflection, to challenge themselves as to whether they are self-centred or outward-focused. The story is also a favourite amongst Christians to use when talking about showing love and compassion for their neighbours, whether they are Christian or not. What the majority of Christians do not realise is that some Jews hear this story as an offensive denigration of Jews. Since the first two characters ignore the man who is mugged, most Jews hear it as being of deliberately anti-Semitic intent, told to foster anti-Semitism even. The question is, would they explain this to Christians? Some who are combative by nature might do so, but the more reserved would not.

I have developed particularly close relationships with a number of Jews through my work at the Centre. One particular individual does share her reaction to this story with Christians on a regular basis, especially as part of the St Philip's Centre training sessions for Christian clergy. They are normally quite taken aback to discover that the story can be heard in that way, but they invariably learn from the encounter. In conversation with this individual, I learned that it was only because of the relationship of trust that I had built up with her that she felt able to first share her views. Trust is crucial for meaningful co-operation to take place.

6

CO-OPERATE

TOM WILSON

In its early years the St Philip's Centre developed a reputation for interfaith sport. Numerous football and cricket matches were organised, both in Leicester and overseas, notably in Stockholm (Sweden) and Berlin (Germany). One finding from this was that imams tend to be younger (and fitter!) than Anglican vicars, with many of the matches ending in a clear Muslim victory over Christians. Not that this mattered at all, except perhaps to the super-competitive, as the point of the sports matches was not the winning but the taking part.

This is a cliché that is regularly used in relation to sporting competitions, especially by the losing side, but, in this case, it was in fact the main aim. The point was not to see whether Christians or Muslims were better at sport but rather to provide an opportunity for people who would not normally encounter each other to do so in a relatively relaxed, informal, non-pressured environment, so that understanding and trust could develop. Ultimately, the aim of all the interfaith sport was to foster co-operation between people who did not otherwise have a reason to co-operate.

Some forms of interfaith co-operation may be very locally based. At other times, it may be tackling much more complex issues, such as child sexual exploitation or hate crime, across a city or wider region. This chapter has two brief case studies of co-operation on child sexual exploitation and hate crime, followed by an in-depth discussion of the Near Neighbours programme.

CASE STUDY 6.1: CHILD SEXUAL EXPLOITATION

In 2015 the St Philip's Centre was approached by the statutory agencies that are responsible for tackling child sexual exploitation in Leicester, Leicestershire and Rutland. They had noticed that there was a statistical under-reporting of child sexual exploitation particularly amongst ethnic minority and faith communities. This is not necessarily to say that there is a problem of child sexual exploitation within those communities, but simply that there is a statistical anomaly, which suggests there might be a problem. Those in the City and County Council and the police who have responsibility for dealing with the reality of child sexual exploitation recognised the importance of working with others in order to determine whether the anomaly was indicative of a problem that was not being addressed.

The St Philip's Centre was central to the initial work in this area in relation to some of the faith communities. Since we are a resourcing, not a representative, organisation, we could not speak with the civic authorities on behalf of people of faith. However, we could enable the conversation to begin to take place. In this instance, we needed to both develop understanding and trust before encounter could take place, which in turn would lead to the possibility of co-operation. Understanding and trust were two sides of the same coin in this encounter, primarily because of an incident which occurred in Leicester in 2013. The general concern is especially prevalent within sections of the Hindu and Sikh community, namely that gangs of (Pakistani) Muslim men are targeting girls for grooming and exploitation. A historic issue (whereby Sikh men attacked a Muslim whom they believed to be responsible for grooming a Sikh girl) complicated the situation considerably (BBC 2013b). The Sikh, and to some extent Muslim and Hindu, communities all had concerns over how the police had handled this issue, resulting in a lack of confidence in the ability of the police to tackle as complex an issue as child sexual exploitation with appropriate sensitivity. It was therefore important to help everyone involved understand the perspective of the others who were involved and to develop appropriate bonds of trust.

We managed to do this to some extent. The notable success was the agreement that we would hold a public seminar that raised the issues and suggested strategies for tackling them. This face-to-face encounter was aimed at developing co-operation between different faith groups and statutory agencies, allowing them to start tackling a complex and difficult problem. Although the initial seminar took place and was well received, at the time of writing a tender was reissued by Leicestershire County Council to deliver a bespoke awareness programme for the faith communities.

CASE STUDY 6.2: HATE CRIME

One of the particular challenges for the St Philip's Centre is the complexity of *intra*faith relations, in particular determining where those boundaries lie. Many religions are complex, and it is not always straightforward determining who actually is a member of any particular religion. Thus, are Messianic Jews (that is, those who follow Jewish practices but recognise Jesus as Messiah) to be regarded as Jews or as Christians? Similarly, are Jehovah's Witnesses a Christian group? Are the Ahmadiyyas to be recognised as Muslim? This series of questions could continue for other faith traditions (as noted in an earlier chapter), but the status of the Ahmadiyya community is of particular relevance to the discussion of hate crime.

According to a recent report from the organisation Faith Matters, 2016 saw a significant increase in incidents of hate crime against the Ahmadiyya community, rising from nine in 2015 to 29 in 2016 (Faith Matters 2016, p.3). Of particular concern is the murder of Glasgow shopkeeper Asad Shah by a Muslim, Tanver Ahmed, who believed he was professing to be a prophet. Ahmed stated in court that Shah had 'disrespected Islam' and that this was a capital crime (Johnson 2016). A personality cult has developed around Tanver Ahmed, praising him for his actions, which appear to be motivated, at least in part, by the murder of Pakistani politician Salman Taseer by his bodyguard Mumtaz Qadri in 2011.

The debate as to whether Ahmadiyyas are Muslim is a fraught one, and not an issue the St Philip's Centre is qualified to comment on. The implications for our work are complex. We aim to work with all faith groups, and those of no faith who are relevant to us (for example, with the Leicester Secular Society). But the reality is that, if we were to regularly invite members of Leicester's Ahmadiyya community to interfaith gatherings, others would then choose to not attend. I have experienced personal pressure and criticism for attending the opening of Masjid Baitul Ikram, the Ahmadiyya mosque.

This experience of criticism for working with minority groups on the fringe of a religion is not unique to Islam. Similar questions have been raised over our work with ISKCON and Swaminarayan Hindus, as well as more recent engagement with the Mormons. For us, the question is of attitude and disposition. Do we knowingly exclude, or do we strive to include as best as we can, whilst also recognising the pragmatic decisions that must be made in the real world? We endeavour to do the latter, as far as we are able.

Thus in the aftermath of the EU referendum we hosted a public meeting on responding to the increase in hate crime that has been widely documented. We continue to work with the police on developing programmes for educating perpetrators of hate crime. And we continue to build relationships with communities whom others choose to ignore.

Near Neighbours
Background
The Near Neighbours programme works to bring people together who are near neighbours in communities that are religiously and ethnically diverse, so that they can get to know each other better, build relationships of trust and co-operate together on initiatives that improve the local community they live in. The programme has two key objectives. The first is social interaction: to develop positive relationships in multifaith areas. That is, to help people of different faiths and ethnicities get to know and understand each other better. The second is social action: to encourage people of different faiths and of no faith to come together for initiatives that improve their local neighbourhood. The underlying philosophy is that it is local people, in local communities, who are the ones who are ideally placed to identify and develop solutions that can improve their own neighbourhood. The aim is to bring people together, to break down misunderstanding and develop trust, helping people to act to change their communities for the better.

The programme is funded by the UK Department for Communities and Local Government (DCLG) and centrally administered by the Church Urban Fund (CUF), working locally through a number of hubs. There have been a number of rounds of funding for Near Neighbours. At the time of writing, the programme is in receipt of the third round of funding, for a single financial year (2016/17), and works in eight regions of England. These are: East London; West London; Luton; East Midlands, covering Leicester and Nottingham; Birmingham; the Black Country, covering Dudley, Smethwick, Walsall and Sandwell; Greater Manchester, which includes Prestwich, Bury, Rochdale and Oldham; and West Yorkshire, covering Bradford, Leeds and Dewsbury. The eight regional hubs act as focal points for much of the work of the programme. There is a co-ordinator based at each, who connects with local projects, develops the work of the programme and develops, strengthens and deepens networks and action amongst local communities in their region. Near Neighbours is also linked with a number of national partners. These include The Feast, Catalyst, the Three Faiths Forum, the Christian–Muslim forum, the Hindu–Christian forum and the Council of Christians and Jews, all of which gather people together to develop understandings and relationships and to work for the common good.

One of the main areas of work within the Near Neighbours programme is the small grants fund. It offers seed capital of between £250 and £5000 for local groups and organisations who are working to bring neighbours together, to develop relationships of diverse faiths and ethnicities and to improve communities. The grants are open to anyone who meets the three criteria by which grants are assessed. First, projects should create association. The aim is to encourage a stronger civil society in areas that are multi-religious and multi-ethnic by creating association, friendship and neighbourliness. The project must therefore be a partnership between at least two organisations who are neighbours in some sense. Second, the project should be local and sustainable. Grants should be spent in ways which bring together people from different ethnic and faith communities which impact specifically locally, with relationships continuing naturally beyond the initial funding. Third, projects should be transformative. Neighbourhoods where projects run should be better places as a result. This may be as simple as litter picking or as complex as reducing tension between different communities in a particular neighbourhood.

In the first two rounds, the Near Neighbours grants fund awarded seed capital worth £3.66 million to over 1120 projects. These projects impacted the lives of 941,000 people, and 71 per cent of them continued to run after the initial seed capital was spent. In Leicester alone 102 local neighbourhood projects have been funded, with a total of just over £267,000 awarded to the groups in the city. Nottingham was part of the second phase, and over 40 projects have received just under £153,000 in grants. Two examples of projects funded are described below.

Examples

SaSh

Salaam Shalom (SaSh) Kitchen is a joint initiative of Nottingham's Liberal Synagogue in partnership with Himmah, a Muslim social action charity. Launched on 6 May 2015, it provides a weekly drop-in kitchen for the city's poorest and most vulnerable people. Using the United Reformed Church-owned Bridge Community Centre in the Hyson Green area of the city, volunteers from both faiths work together to offer friendship and hot food to people of any faith or no faith who live locally and are in need. Local chefs help prepare the meals, which are made from donated produce. One of the co-founders, Sajid Mohammed, explained the rationale behind the project: 'In the past 12 months we have seen a rise in Islamophobia and anti-Semitism. Nottingham has for the most part been quite sheltered, but we felt that now is the right moment to give hope and demonstrate our communities' values of compassion, dignity and care for others.'

Festival of Season's Greetings

St Mary's Church in Humberstone in Leicester held a festival that all could take part in. It was called a Festival of Season's Greetings, so that each faith could show how they celebrated their religious festivals. Invitations went out through local contacts, and a small grant from Near Neighbours covered the cost of food, decorations and publicity. Stalls for each faith were set up in the church hall. Small exhibitions, demonstrations, activities and food tasting were all on offer, and over 200 people came to enjoy each other's company and learn more about each other's beliefs.

Case studies

Below are two further examples of the types of projects that have been funded. Projects were asked to provide case study information, and each responded in a different way. They have been left largely as received, in order to better demonstrate the wide variety of work supported.

CASE STUDY 6.3: MAMMAS (ORIGINALLY WESLEY HALL MAMMAS)

Sally Etheridge was a prime motivator in creating the Mammas Project. She is an International Board Certified lactation consultant, but her wonderfully calm and approachable manner is perhaps the most successful attribute in her determination to help mums and babies thrive. The project supports new mothers and breastfeeding families in the very ethnically diverse Highfields and surrounding neighbourhoods of Leicester. Particularly but not exclusively targeting mothers born outside of the UK, Mammas was set up in 2009 as a Community Breastfeeding Peer Support project.

The project was meeting in the Wesley Hall Methodist Church when it heard about Near Neighbours (NN). An application to NN from an existing organisation such as the Mammas is not normally a high priority, with preference being given to new and emergent initiatives. However, it strongly met key criteria in bringing people of different faiths and ethnicities together for the first time, helping them cope with disadvantage and build lasting relationships across faiths. Being based in the Highfields area ticked enough boxes for NN, and in 2012 a grant of £3831 was awarded to the Mammas committee of nine mothers, amongst whom were representatives of Islam, Judaism, Christianity, Hinduism and Atheism.

Based on a community consultation, the group planned to expand the number of peer supporters it co-ordinated to meet the level of need, and tackle isolation within the community. The project trained eight new peer mentors, delivered six antenatal breastfeeding sessions, and set up a weekly friendship group for new mothers, working in partnership with the local SureStart centre. The grant funded training costs, sessional fees, venue hire and volunteer expenses. Successive NN grants have been awarded to help Mammas develop new initiatives with a wide range of other new mums. Sally suggests that the funding from NN has given other funders the confidence to support the project. And through Sally's professional contacts the project links with and advises other projects across the world.

Mammas works via an early intervention model to reduce health inequalities, social deprivation and isolation among new mothers, signposting to other services such as midwives, health visitors, SureStart, community centres and schools, receiving referrals, sessions, education and information. Following NN funding they have successfully gained an award of £19,000 over two years from the People's Health Trust and further support from the Feminist Review Trust. The new All Party Parliamentary Group on Infant Feeding has invited Sally to its meetings, and she has been able to offer well-received evidence from the Mammas experience.

Over 60 community mothers have been trained as Mammas, and currently around 30 are active. They use 30 languages, including British Sign Language (BSL), and now run a Community Breastfeeding Helpline 'Mammaline' 9am–9pm every day, plus a dedicated Gujarati and Urdu Mammaline. The project offers home visits to most new mothers in the Spinney Hill and Evington areas of Leicester, many of whom for cultural reasons stay in the home for 40 days following birth. The project runs 'Feeding Your New Baby' antenatal classes at Wesley Hall Community Centre and also delivered 'Start of Something Special' antenatal classes on 'feeding your new baby' across SureStart centres in central neighbourhoods of the city.

Telephone postnatal follow-up was especially appropriate. Around three quarters of new mothers were successfully contacted, of which approximately one quarter come to one of the Mammas groups. Two successful, well-evaluated postnatal mother and baby sessions were offered within the community, with 60 women receiving weekly text reminders. The project recognises the role of the extended family and developed 'Dear Grandparents' leaflets, aiming to reduce cultural pressure to 'top-up' with a bottle feed.

The project has matured in both its ability and its organisational skills and has become a Community Interest

Company run by mums for mums, and delivers ongoing training and supervision for Mamma Peer Supporters, including help in moving on to work. The project has developed Disclosure and Barring Service (DBS) and safeguarding policies amongst other standards, and this is being recognised by stakeholders and funders as a quality assurance that the mums can be proud of.

The following information has been supplied by the Mammas to illustrate their work:

» Service users: our Mammas Baby & Me group, which is for mums and their babies to get info, support and friendship, meets in two children's centres, and now we also arrange visits which are very popular.

» Swimming for mums and babies: on a freezing day we had eight mums and babies, some had not been to a pool since childhood and were very anxious. One mum said before the visit, 'My baby is eight months old, just thinking of bringing her, but I'm no good at swimming, not been in a pool since I was at school.' After the visit she said, 'Yep, it was a lovely day at swimming; really enjoyed it. Yep, if you did it again, then we would come, she fell asleep straight away when we got home.'

» Visit to New Walk Museum in summer 2016. They had 21 parents and babies, most had never been to the museum.

» Fun Valley Soft Play, visit in August 2016 had 18 mums and babies.

» These visits are a good way to meet our objectives of reducing social isolation, offering evidence-based info about infant feeding and baby concerns, and giving one-to-one support.

> » We set up a WhatsApp group, and now have 180 mums chatting to one another. We moderate and ensure the info is appropriate and can call mums individually if there is an obvious cause for concern, or contact a mum to encourage her to come to a group and meet others.

> » A weekly text message is sent out to 350 mothers.

> » Our baby massage groups enabled by NN have also brought mums together. Fifteen attended the two pilot courses, and we are about to begin three more courses, which will include mums referred by health visitors.

> » Mums are from all social and economic backgrounds: 95 per cent have a black or minority ethnic (BME) background.

'Zara', a young mum of a four-month-old, said, 'Thank you so much for being there and for being very supportive. I think I was able to push myself because you were giving me encouraging words which I really needed at that time.'

'Farzana' said, 'I just wanted you to know that you were a great help to us, and I wish I had met more people like you during my pregnancy and after.'

CASE STUDY 6.4: ONE ROOF LEICESTER

Mrs Salma Ravat is a dedicated family woman who has a busy home life and yet still found time to volunteer in inspirational ways to help some of the most disadvantaged people in Leicester. She is inspired by her Islamic faith to offer non-conditional support and care to those around her and particularly to the homeless who often fall through the net of statutory responsibility. Working through the good offices of the Islamic Society of Britain's (ISB) Leicester Branch, Salma sought a meeting alongside her women colleagues from ISB to meet Near Neighbours co-ordinator John McCallum in 2011. This meeting explained the learning Salma and her friends were gaining in supplying donated foodstuffs, toiletries and clothing to vulnerable people regardless of race, faith or background.

Concerned that their activity was not meeting the needs of some of the people they met, Salma and her team sought help from Near Neighbours to get more people involved in supporting the homeless of many faiths and ethnicities they were meeting. Following this meeting she approached the Vicar of St James the Greater Anglican Church on London Road, Canon Glynn Richerby, and asked if she and fellow Muslim volunteers might work with the church to create a project on Saturdays. The women had realised that, even in the winter, many agencies closed for the weekend, and with the dramatically rising numbers of homeless people in Leicester many of them might have to spend the day in the cold and go unfed. With the willing agreement of the church to use their premises and also to provide volunteers from the congregation, the Eat'n'Meet Project, which evolved into the Saturday Stop By Project, was created. Near Neighbours helped it launch with a small grant of £3200 for six months' activity. Five years on, this important work now sees numerous homeless people spending a few hours in warm and friendly company and getting a hot meal and cup of tea as well as being able to share their problems and sometimes seek further help from the network of contacts Salma and the team have built up. The Stop By team is increasingly diverse, with many folk who are neither Muslim nor Christian offering their time to support the work.

In her quiet and courteous manner Salma has not let that be the limit of her ambitions to help vulnerable people, as she quickly realised that, although there were a number of voluntary agencies working with the homeless in the city, they did not regularly meet together or have truly co-ordinated activity. In her typically friendly way Salma simply asked the people she met from the agencies to come along to meetings hosted by Near Neighbours in the St Philip's Centre and discuss with her and other volunteers their joint concerns about the homeless. Their first meeting was a great success and led to a visionary organisation, the Leicester Homeless Forum, and latterly One Roof Leicester, of which Salma became the lead worker.

One Roof Leicester (ORL) is a consortium of independent faith, community and voluntary sector organisations supporting the homeless, destitute and vulnerably housed in Leicester. The founding partner organisations are Community of Grace, the Centre Project, the Anglican Diocese of Leicester and the Islamic Society of Britain. In 2012 they identified the need to work more closely together, to ensure there was daily provision for all homeless people, especially those sleeping rough, and to avoid duplication of services. ORL Partners have been supporting people affected by homelessness for over 40 years by providing daily hot meals, advice, mentoring, social activities, education and/or accommodation. ORL also promotes and raises awareness within the wider community about homelessness issues. They deliver workshops in schools, talks for faith and community groups, provide support to organisations and individuals wanting to set up new projects, and advise those who want to be actively involved. In December 2016 they launched what they claim to be Britain's first multifaith winter night shelter (Sherwood 2016a). Throughout the winter, seven faith organisations opened their doors to provide shelter, warmth and hospitality to ten rough sleepers each night. From 12 December 2016 to 27 February 2017, each venue offered weekly accommodation, supported by volunteers of all faiths and none, from across the city.

7

INTERFAITH IN THE TWENTY-FIRST CENTURY

RIAZ RAVAT

This book has outlined how the place and role of religion and belief in contemporary UK society is increasingly being contested. How we live together well and handle the differences between our neighbours and ourselves is highly salient in political and faith circles.

Most people in the UK want to get on with their lives and live in peace with their neighbours. According to Katwala, 83 per cent of those surveyed fully agreed and only 3 per cent disagreed with the following statement about integration: 'To belong to our shared society, everyone must speak our language, obey our laws and pay their taxes – so that everyone who plays by the rules counts as equally British and should be able to reach their potential' (Katwala 2014, p.16). People want access to quality services to meet basic human needs plus a strong economy, good government and a society where they are valued for who they are and what they can contribute. They want a degree of liberty and freedom so that they can make their own choices and want their views and beliefs about the world to be respected. They want order, fairness and justice maintained by the rule of law. They want to live in a society of balance between opposing views, where no one group dominates and where conflicts are resolved peacefully. 'The overwhelming majority of us believe in treating people fairly and with respect, no matter what their background' (Department for Communities and Local Government (DCLG) 2012, p.3). Such principles provide the basis of our liberal democracy and the social contract which our nation rests on.

Not everyone, however, sees their place in society in this way. There are ways of thinking and acting which actively or passively disapprove of such values and work against them by promoting discrimination and inequality. They brook no opposition and privilege their own vision over the rights and freedoms of others. At the heart of such thinking is a superiority complex which creates a polarised climate of distrust and suspicion that can lead to isolation, separation and, worse still, hate and violence.

Catalyst

Catalyst is the Centre's flagship young adults' life skills and leadership programme formed as a result of the Near Neighbours initiative. Incidentally, as far back as 2004, I wrote a report which argued that a programme which specifically funded initiatives to bring together two or more communities for face-to-face encounter was required (Ravat 2004, pp.37–9). At the time, there were schemes which adopted a more single community focus. Near Neighbours in 2011 realised this recommendation. The Cantle report (Cantle 2001) also criticised single community funding for fuelling divisions which led to the riots in several northern English areas.

Catalyst has been delivered by the Centre to young people in Leicester, Luton, Nottingham and London, with further programmes run in the West Midlands, the northwest and Yorkshire by other partners. Delivered well, it can make a considerable contribution to addressing some of the integration challenges noted in this book and by Casey (Casey 2016).

When the Catalyst programme was first put together, I was insistent that it had to stretch boundaries in many ways and needed to be relevant. Key to this were comments from the director-general of the Confederation of British Industry (CBI) that the education system needs to develop more holistic young people. In 2014 John Cridland was reported to have said: 'Schools need to teach character to children and be judged on this by Ofsted.' He added that 'schools were too focused on exam results and should teach pupils resilience and how to be rounded and grounded' (Woolcock 2014).

Subsequently, he went on to say, 'You differentiate by character. Character attributes and behaviours are equally as important as qualifications' (Schools Improvement 2015). This is exactly what Catalyst is based on. The programme equips young adults with essential life skills. It is encounter based and inspiring. It builds character and confidence, and encourages critical thinking. The package offers vital, practical skills for young people as they navigate through society whether in education, work or part of community life. Catalyst adds value to existing post-16 provision and ably prepares tomorrow's generation. Catalyst is accredited by Leicester College and operates at three levels – bronze, silver and gold. The interactive content covers leadership attributes and styles, presentation and communication skills, decision-making, running community projects, personal finance, equality and interfaith understanding.

On this last point, Catalyst provides an opportunity to learn about religious and non-religious beliefs, but it is not a leadership programme to churn out faith leaders. This is a crucial point because, by opening the doors to participation, communities which can be described as the 'white underclass', African Caribbean boys, Pakistani and Bangladeshi females, orthodox Jews and Hindu and Sikh females have all completed Catalyst. To differing degrees, some of them have been noted as 'hard to reach'. By working with educational institutions, a diverse mix of participants has been sought.

One of the pioneering aspects of Catalyst is that those who deliver on the programme come from a variety of personal and professional backgrounds. Rather than playing it safe, the programme stretches boundaries by creating a genuine and open platform for learning. Those who deliver sessions include colleagues who have experience of working in education, the police, armed forces, politics and pro-equality campaigns, including sexual orientation.

Innovation is a recurrent theme. Catalyst avoids a 'classroom'-based approach where presenters simply impart information and participants absorb this. Sessions are interactive and creative, where case studies, teamwork or entrepreneurial skills are required.

In a UK of increasing diversity, Catalyst has still led to many first-time encounters. This exposure-based method of promoting diversity bypasses many filters. Catalyst has authored many ground-breaking and life-changing stories such as young Hindus, Muslims and Sikhs meeting a rabbi and a Buddhist monk, where the Baha'i faith has been revealed, and where Humanism is given a platform alongside religion – all under the stewardship of Church of England structures which have enabled the established church to play a leadership role in modern, diverse, community life. Catalyst has created alternative narratives and an ethos which recognises diversity within the parameters of a cohesive community.

The impact of Catalyst upon its beneficiaries cannot be overstated. Religious literacy is an important pillar of the programme but not the only one. Young Muslim females have particularly remarked on their levels of confidence increasing. Sharmina Uddin, a young Muslim female of Bangladeshi heritage, said:

> This programme has empowered me to become more assertive and find inner confidence and self-belief inside – qualities that I can use to achieve my full potential. Before I was a person who used to hide, but that is no longer the case.

Rahoul Naik, a male Hindu participant, added:

> The biggest thing it [Catalyst] opened my eyes to was how to approach people. The line of work that I currently do and the line I aim to pursue requires a huge amount of personal skills and the ability to speak to anyone. I now understand how different people react, how people think depending on their backgrounds and the best way to approach them.

Catalyst promotes the common good and gives young people the confidence and capacity to respond to the challenges they face whether in the job market or in their personal, social and religious lives. Graduates complete the programme knowing that the world is more complex than the polarised, bipartisan picture which is all too often painted. They see this nuance as a strength that when you take identity variables into consideration, such as race, gender, disability, religion or belief, sexuality, language and culture, human beings have more in correlation with each other than the separate, single identity prism which those who wish to divide us present. Catalyst seeks to 'create more opportunities for people to come together and understand what they hold in common and for people to use these shared values to develop partnerships which bring about real and positive change with their local community' (DCLG 2008, p.21). We are all stronger together.

Social action days

The St Philip's Centre has helped to reshape interfaith
work by developing innovative, accessible opportunities
which reach a wider audience. Since 2010, there have been
noticeable efforts by national faith bodies to co-ordinate
service-based volunteering. Sewa Day, Mitzvah Day,
Interfaith Iftaars and 'A Year of Service' are just some of
the programmes we have delivered with partners in the
faith communities. Such initiatives have broadened the
way in which encounter takes place. Whether standing
in solidarity outside supermarkets on freezing Sundays in
November to collect toiletries for the homeless or running
tea parties for the elderly, the creation of such wholesome
and open dialogical encounters creates the basis from
which insecurity can be replaced by inclusion and where
reservations are converted to relationships.

To sustain interfaith harmony we need to create more
arenas to act as places of encounter for dialogue. Diversity
over uniformity is a given, but the more we separate in our
minds, the more we segregate in our hearts. Whether we are
policy makers, opinion formers, service providers or indeed
communities, we need to robustly assess the impact of our
actions for the universal golden rules of treating others as
we would want to be treated ourselves and to impart and
attribute respect and incalculable value on all of humanity.

Mitzvah Day and Sewa Day are two days fixed in the
annual life of the St Philip's Centre. 'Mitzvah' means a 'good
deed' in Hebrew, whilst 'Sewa' originates from the Indian
language of Sanskrit and the concept invokes a spirit of
community and selfless service for a just and fair society.
The core beliefs of both days are the same – to sacrifice
your time and resources for the benefit of others without
wanting anything in return.

Leicester would not be Leicester unless we delivered
Mitzvah Day or Sewa Day in our own unique and

cosmopolitan style. This is why for us each day is anchored in the wider interfaith context of the city. It is all too easy to run campaigns for individual faiths, by individual faiths. Rather, we have established special partnerships which include synagogues, gurdwaras, Hindu groups, a Buddhist temple and an Indian restaurant, as well as individual volunteers from the many faith and belief communities. When Leicester contributes, it makes a difference by being different.

Examples of our actions have included entertaining tea parties for elderly members of the African Caribbean community, Muslims, Sikhs, Hindus and white deprived groups from Syston in Leicestershire. Other work has included collecting essential supplies from shoppers to then donate to charities supporting victims of domestic violence. Our vision is that not only are we 'doing good' for society's most isolated and vulnerable groups but we are also building relational bridges between people of different backgrounds, both between the volunteers themselves and also with the wider public.

Mitzvah Day and Sewa Day serve as reminders about the long-standing contributions made by Jews, Buddhists, Hindus and Sikhs to the social fabric of the UK. Charity is part and parcel of these major faiths and is delivered in places of worship and communities every single day of the week. The St Philip's Centre with its Christian heritage has co-ordinated these distinctive efforts.

Sceptics would argue that these sorts of initiatives are tokenistic and of limited value, but try telling that to one of the elderly ladies who said that our presence made her feel 'royal', or the shopper who was once a victim of domestic violence who told us that we must 'keep going because there is still so much of this violence happening today'. For those at the forefront, our efforts are welcome and worthy. We are now entering a period when a realignment of culture and thinking on matters interfaith is being pushed by policy makers. There is still scope for public endorsement of single faith activities because of the recognition of considerable internal diversity, but this is no longer seen in the same way. There is a greater emphasis on bridge-building initiatives and stepping out of one's comfort zone.

Former Prime Minister David Cameron termed this the 'Big Society', but many years ago in the city of Leicester, my 2004 report, *Embracing the Present, Planning the Future* calculated the £5 million contribution faith-based volunteers were making to social action through their time (Ravat 2004). The St Philip's Centre has for a long time pioneered a number of interfaith initiatives from education to encounter and sport to social action. The world of interfaith dialogue must seize this opportunity to innovate and carve out different ways in how we 'do interfaith'. Innovation in approach enables us to reach out to others not yet involved, and inclusion in method enables us to remain true to the principles of all of our faiths.

Interfaith relations take place in many forms and guises, from the formal structured conversations between leaders to the informal encounters between people in supermarkets or at the school gates. The word 'encounter' is central to promoting an environment where interfaith relations can flourish. However, the continued success of interfaith relations requires new tools as we get to grips with the increased richness of the tapestry which makes up the UK.

In 2013, in an act of immense humility, Pope Francis washed and kissed the feet of 12 prisoners, one of them a Muslim inmate. As the global leader of an estimated 1.2 billion Roman Catholics, his actions demonstrated that immersion in one faith need not restrict the deliverance of virtue.

In 2011 Pope Francis as Cardinal Bergoglio wrote the following compelling words:

> Dialogue is born from an attitude of respect for the other person, from a conviction that the other person has something good to say. It assumes that there is room in the heart for the person's point of view, opinion, and proposal. To dialogue entails a cordial reception, not a prior condemnation. In order to dialogue it is necessary to know how to lower the defenses, open the doors of the house, and offer human warmth. (United States Conference of Catholic Bishops (USCCB) 2013, p.1)

8

WHERE NEXT?

TOM WILSON

We need to move to beyond inter-religious interaction in which we the usual suspects issue bland statements of anaemic intent – with which you could paper the walls of Lambeth Palace, and much good would it do you – all desperate to agree with one another, so that the very worst outcome could possibly be that we end up acknowledging our differences.

That is not enough in the face of the dangers we face at this time. It is disingenuous and ultimately dishonest, because alongside all that we hold in common and all that we share, there are profound differences too in what we believe and in the outworking of our faith. True friendships and relationships can withstand honestly held differences in values, opinions and religious understandings, and a common commitment to mutual flourishing in diversity. (Welby 2015)

We live in an uncertain world, where religiously motivated violence is an increasing threat. Division, hatred and mistrust dominate. What, if anything, can we do about it? This chapter argues that a few simple steps are needed. We must first acknowledge what is; second, imagine what could be; and third, set about realising that vision. Each step is simple to outline, but difficult to achieve.

Acknowledging what is

The first step in realising change is to acknowledge the reality of the situation in which we find ourselves. We may, or may not, want to be where we are, but we are where we are, and no amount of pretending or protesting will change that simple fact. Complaining or embracing the mentality of victimhood may have a degree of catharsis but it will not bring about lasting solutions or change. The sooner we come to accept the reality of our present situation, the sooner we are able to bring about change.

There are many aspects of modern British society that we at the St Philip's Centre have concerns about, and we will discuss four of them here. These are: first, the lack of available resource; second, the tendency to embrace victimhood over action; third, hatred within and between communities; and fourth, the threat of terrorist and/or extremist action. Each will be examined in turn.

It is a truism of any discussion of problems that the resources available are insufficient to meet the scale of the challenge. This is as true within inter- and intrafaith engagement as elsewhere. The recent austerity years have meant that relatively little resource is devoted to raising religious literacy amongst workforces. Leicestershire County Council (LCC), for example, has a budget of £60,000 for interfaith education and activities both amongst its staff and in its public engagement for the financial year 2016/17. This equates to around £9 per head for its over 6000 staff. Given LCC is host to the Leicestershire Inter Faith Forum, which plans an active programme of four meetings and one significant public conference over the course of the financial year, the amount spent on staff will actually be less than

£9 per head. This example is not intended to single LCC out for any particular criticism but rather to acknowledge what is. The reality is that few organisations within the public sector, whether city or county councils, the police, armed forces, education or healthcare professionals, are devoting much of their resources in the area of interfaith engagement. Yet we live in an increasingly interconnected world, where problems often arise because of simple misunderstandings. Preventative, pre-emptive educative work would greatly reduce this, and this would arguably be a more cost-effective way of acting, as preventing problems is invariably cheaper than taking remedial action afterwards.

The lack of resource is not simply evident in the decreasing budgets of public (and private) sector organisations. It is also true in the day-to-day engagement between people of different faiths. This work is complex, time-consuming and energy intensive, and although richly rewarding is also fraught with challenges, misunderstandings and difficulties. Busy people struggle to make enough time to make it happen. In Leicester, we at the St Philip's Centre are taking steps to equip and resource emerging leaders to be better equipped to engage in this complex work. We hope we can ensure a net increase in the number of leaders, as this is partly a reactive programme, devised in response to the increasing age of some of those involved in our work.

Turning second to the tendency to embrace victimhood over action, the example of car parking is an illustrative, if somewhat tongue-in-cheek, example. In my experience, in the course of interfaith engagements, every faith community will, at some point, mention car parking and explain how they are particular victims of traffic wardens. Whether they are Sikh, Hindu, Muslim or Christian, I have had many conversations about the challenge of parking close to a place of worship, the fact that other communities do not seem to be ticketed as frequently, and so forth. This is, of course, a sweeping (and not especially serious) generalisation. However, it does illustrate a willingness to embrace the status of victim somewhat too quickly. There is a certain comfort in being a victim, as it means problems are not yours to solve – they are down to someone else. Of course, not everyone in every community does this by any means, but it is noticeable that when problems are discussed in an open forum, the conversation can quickly degenerate into competitive victimhood rather than proactive exploration of possible solutions. This observation is not offered as condemnation but as recognition of reality and as a rallying cry, encouraging people who want to work for solutions to become involved.

Before the 2015 General Election in the UK, activist Andy Flannagan edited a book aimed at Christians entitled *Those Who Show Up* (2015). The basic premise was that those who show up, that is, those who take active steps to engage with political processes, are those who influence them and change them. The same is true for any area of life. If we want a society where people learn to live well together, then that will only happen if we take active steps to model that living together and to demonstrate our belief by both word and action. We cannot simply be victims. Even if we have suffered greatly, change will only come when we act to bring it about.

Third, we must acknowledge the reality that there is real tension within and between different communities. This should not be overstated, nor misapplied in a sweeping or crude way. Where it does exist, it should be acknowledged. A few examples will suffice to illustrate the point. There is a debate within Hinduism as to whether the ISKCON or Swaminarayan movements count as Hindu or not. This debate is not entirely amicable and at times can result in vitriolic or condemnatory statements. Similarly, the differences between Sunni and Shi'a Muslims are in theory primarily theological but they can become poisonous, as we have seen in the Middle East. I have heard of a British-based Sunni cleric describing Shi'a Muslims as a 'cancer on Islam' and of Shi'a Muslims being as disparaging about Sunnis. Furthermore, the Ahmadiyya movement is beyond the pale for many Sunni Muslims. Christians can be as harsh towards each other; some hardline Protestants would not recognise Roman Catholics as Christians, for example.

Moreover, there is considerable distrust between faith communities. Some within the Hindu community, for example, have very little time for Christians, suggesting that they have a secret agenda to force conversion and destroy Hindu identity. To give one example: Stephen Crabb's decision to stand for the leadership of the Conservative Party in June 2016 meant his Christian faith was subject to some withering criticism from a Hindu who views all Christian organisations as extremists with a specific agenda to destroy Hindu identity (Hindu Human Rights (HHR) 2016). Some Sikhs are very distrustful of the Muslim community; perhaps at least in part because Sikhs have been victims of Islamophobic attacks (Dart 2016). This observation is not making a point about a problem within a particular faith but the reality of problems within all faiths that, for some, difference is something to be celebrated but, for others, it is something that is feared or even hated. It is sometimes argued that prejudice is the bastion of the old, but our experience is that this is not necessarily true. Many younger people have views which can be described as deeply bigoted. According to an in-depth survey by the University of Leicester involving 1421 respondents who had been victims of hate crime, 7 out of 10 of victims' most recent experiences had been perpetrated by male offenders and a similar proportion had been perpetrated by offenders aged 30 or under. That is to say, hate crime tends to be committed by men under the age of 30 (Chakroborti,

Garland and Hardy 2014, p.54). This is not a problem that is about to go away.

Indeed, fourth, this hatred can become the motivation for extreme, violent or even terrorist behaviour. The murder of Glasgow shopkeeper Asad Shah, discussed earlier, is a case in point. This is but one small example of how hatred can spill over into violence. Often it may remain at the level of hatred, but sometimes it can become the basis for violence.

Four problems have been outlined, but this is not the total of what is. Those who hate may be a vocal minority but they are only a small minority. Some people do want to live with neighbours who have a life journey, background and experience which is different to theirs. The challenge is to ensure that the narrative of living well together becomes far more powerful than that of division and discord.

There are many organisations encouraging people to speak out and to act in solidarity with those who are suffering. The St Philip's Centre is just a very small part of a much wider whole, but we can and will play our part and expect many others to join with us in doing so.

Imagining what could be

The first stage is to acknowledge what is. The second is to imagine what could be. This is not merely an exercise in daydreaming. It is serious, pragmatic planning for the future. At the St Philip's Centre, we imagine a future with these elements: a procedurally pluralist and welcoming public square, a space of good disagreement, and difference becoming a catalyst for growth.

A procedurally pluralist public square is one where many voices have equal access but where no one voice is privileged to the detriment of others. Currently, secular liberal Humanism, with a gradually fading vestige of Anglican

Christian state religion, is the single prevailing, dominant voice in the public square. The Church of England does still have the role of state religion of England, at least, but there are places where standard Anglican teaching is at odds with the prevailing mood of the country and church attendance continues to decline, hence the description of a gradually fading vestige.

The clearest example of variance in teaching concerns human sexuality. Whilst the state recognises the right of any two consenting adults to legally marry, the Church of England continues to teach that marriage can only be between a man and a woman. It is a moot point whether everyone who self-identifies as an Anglican agrees with this teaching, and there is considerable debate as to whether this changes whether 'Anglican' is defined as 'self-identified, whether practising or not' or 'attending church more than twice a month'. Whilst a newspaper article taking the former view of Anglican identity suggests most Anglicans are in favour of same sex marriage (Sherwood 2016b), others would disagree (Psephizo 2016). This example concerns daily life. There are plenty of other areas of Church of England teaching which the majority of the UK population disagree with (the status of Jesus as incarnate Son of God whose atoning death is the one perfect sufficient sacrifice, oblation and satisfaction for sins being one prime example). Moreover, recent research into regular attendance at Church of England churches makes it clear that attendance is declining and that this trend will continue for the next few years at least. This raises the question of how long the Anglican Church can claim a privileged status within the religious discourse of the country.

Although it seems that most within the other faith communities support both the idea of an Anglican coronation for the UK's next monarch (Theos 2015) and have no real problem with Anglican bishops sitting in the

House of Lords (Theos 2009), there is considerable disquiet amongst active secularists in relation to both of these points, not to mention the continued role of the Church of England in supporting education establishments.

The secular, liberal Humanist nature of modern British society is seen clearly in the shifts reported in the British Social Attitudes (BSA) Survey. They report that the British public have become far more liberal in their attitudes towards premarital sex since the 1980s. However, the proportion saying extramarital sex is always or mostly wrong has consistently remained above 80 per cent. Views on homosexuality were less tolerant in the early years of the survey, but since the late 1980s have become increasingly liberal. Religious affiliation has declined, with more people now (2015) saying they do not identify with a religion than in 1983 (49 per cent and 31 per cent respectively). Most of this change is accounted for by the decline in affiliation to the Church of England (17 per cent now compared with 40 per cent in 1983) (BSA 2015). The religious landscape of the United Kingdom is developing and becoming increasingly complex. On the one hand, there is a marked increase amongst the 'nones', that is, those who do not identify as belonging to any particular faith tradition. On the other hand, there is also a significant increase in the number of people who are confident in identifying themselves as a person of faith and in expecting to be able to practise their faith confidently and openly in public.

How should these different, competing voices be held in creative tension? A future where all faiths and no faith are given equal voice within the public square, where genuine difference is acknowledged but not condemned, is the only possible solution. This public square is a sophisticated one, as it allows mutually exclusive truth claims equal space without making any form of value judgement over them. Returning to the example of human sexuality noted above, if this public square is genuinely receptive to everyone, it will allow both those who wish to see marriage between any two consenting adults and those who see marriage as exclusively between a man and a woman an equal voice.

How do we get there?

There are many organisations which are working hard to ensure that we are learning to live well together, and the St Philip's Centre is partnering with those we are able to work with. One example of our current work in this area is a partnership with Trade, a LGBT sexual health charity based in Leicester. Recognising the severe mental, social and even, at times, physical pressure that LGBT people of faith face, the two organisations are working together to raise awareness of the issues and develop discussions about appropriate ways forward. Thinking about the project in terms of the four criteria the St Philip's Centre use to evaluate our work, we are seeking to encourage people of differing views to encounter each other and develop genuine, deep understanding of the different perspectives held. We acknowledge that it is unlikely that we will all agree on everything in these discussions, but are working to develop relationships of trust in which we can co-operate to ensure that people are physically, mentally and socially safe.

The vision for an inclusive, welcoming, accepting 'public square' is an attractive one but also one that is very hard to realise. Getting there will require hard work, dedication, commitment, investment of resource and both time and money, and will include many frustrations and challenges. The St Philip's Centre's understanding is that the route is via encounter, understanding, trust and co-operation. As was noted at a number of points throughout the book, this is not necessarily a linear progression. Some people will need to develop trust before they are able to genuinely understand perspectives that are different from their own. Other people may need to first understand the situation of others before they are able to genuinely encounter them. There are many points of departure on this journey towards the future we aspire towards. The route is not important – what is critical is that we set out on the journey.

REFERENCES

Anglo-Sikh Wars (2016) Home page. Leicester: Sikh Museum Initiative. Accessed on 18/01/17 at www.anglosikhwars.com.

Associated Press in Jerusalem (2015) 'Jewish global population approaches pre-Holocaust levels.' *Guardian*, 28 June. Accessed on 19/01/17 at https://www.theguardian.com/world/2015/jun/28/jewish-global-population-approaches-pre-holocaust-levels.

Baldet, W. (2016) 'Prevent isn't just about Islamist extremism – I've worked with a 10-year-old boy already immersed in Nazi culture.' *Independent*, 15 December. Accessed on 20/01/17 at www.independent.co.uk/voices/prevent-far-right-extremism-neo-nazi-white-supremecist-islamic-extremism-a7476906.html.

Bard, M. G. (1998) *Jewish Dietary Laws (Kashrut): Overview of Laws & Regulations.* Jewish Virtual Library website. Accessed on 20/01/17 at www.jewishvirtuallibrary.org/jsource/Judaism/kashrut.html.

BBC (2009a) 'Buddhism and abortion.' Accessed on 18/01/17 at www.bbc.co.uk/religion/religions/buddhism/buddhistethics/abortion.shtml.

BBC (2009b) 'Buddhism and organ donation.' Accessed on 18/01/17 at www.bbc.co.uk/religion/religions/buddhism/buddhistethics/organdonation.shtml.

BBC (2009c) 'Euthanasia, assisted dying and suicide.' Accessed on 18/01/17 at www.bbc.co.uk/religion/religions/hinduism/hinduethics/euthanasia.shtml.

BBC (2009d) 'Abortion.' Accessed on 18/01/17 at www.bbc.co.uk/religion/religions/judaism/jewishethics/abortion_1.shtml.

BBC (2009e) 'Euthanasia, assisted dying and suicide.' Accessed on 18/01/17 at www.bbc.co.uk/religion/religions/sikhism/ sikhethics/euthanasia.shtml.

BBC (2012) 'Euthanasia, assisted dying, suicide, and medical ethics.' Accessed on 18/01/17 at www.bbc.co.uk/religion/ religions/islam/islamethics/euthanasia.shtml.

BBC (2013a) 'British Airways Christian employee Nadia Eweida wins case.' Accessed on 18/01/17 at www.bbc.co.uk/news/uk-21025332.

BBC (2013b) 'Moghul Durbar Leicester restaurant attack: Six arrested.' Accessed on 18/01/17 at www.bbc.co.uk/news/uk-england-leicestershire-21023180.

BBC (2016a) 'Hate crime reports to Leicestershire Police "double" post-EU referendum.' Accessed on 18/01/17 at www.bbc.co.uk/news/uk-england-leicestershire-36697755.

BBC (2016b) 'Theresa May launches race audit of public services.' Accessed on 18/01/17 at www.bbc.co.uk/news/uk-politics-37194207.

BBC (2016c) 'Black Monday: Polish women strike against abortion ban.' Accessed on 18/01/17 at www.bbc.co.uk/news/ world-europe-37540139.

BBC (2016d) '"Prevent" counter-extremism strategy faces legal challenge.' Accessed on 18/01/17 at www.bbc.co.uk/news/uk-38209567.

BBC (2016e) '"Terrorist house" boy "became isolated".' Accessed on 18/01/17 at www.bbc.co.uk/news/uk-england-lancashire-35359410.

Berger, J. M. (2015) 'Tailored online interventions: The Islamic State's recruitment strategy.' *Combating Terrorism Center Sentinel 8*, 10, 19–23.

Bretherton, L. (2010) *Hospitality as Holiness.* Farnham: Ashgate.

BSA (2015) *Explore the British Social Attitudes Survey.* London: NatCen Social Research. Accessed on 19/01/17 at www.bsa-data.natcen.ac.uk.

Cantle, T. (2001) *Community Cohesion: A Report of the Independent Review Team.* London: Home Office.

Casey, L. (2016) *The Casey Review: A Review into Opportunity and Integration.* London: Department for Communities and Local Government.

Census 2011 (n.d.) *Nomis Official Labour Market Statistics.* Accessed on 31/01/17 at www.nomisweb.co.uk/census/2011/ks209ew.

Chakraborti, N., Garland, J. and Hardy, S-J. (2014) *The Leicester Hate Crime Project: Findings and Conclusions.* Leicester: University of Leicester. Accessed on 19/01/17 at https://www2.le.ac.uk/departments/criminology/hate/documents/fc-full-report.

Chakrabortty, A. (2014) 'Narendra Modi, a man with a massacre on his hands, is not the reasonable choice for India.' *Guardian,* 7 April. Accessed on 19/01/17 at https://www.theguardian.com/commentisfree/2014/apr/07/narendra-modi-massacre-next-prime-minister-india.

Chauhan, S. (2014) 'Sikh farmers in Gujarat.' *India Today,* 25 March. Accessed on 20/01/17 at http://indiatoday.intoday.in/story/sikh-farmers-kutch-narendra-modi-akali-dal-bjp-aam-aadmi-party-congress-bombay-land-and-tenancy-act/1/351179.html.

Cole, S. (2016) 'Hear us out before you knock Prevent – we're trying to save lives.' *Guardian,* 31 October. Accessed on 19/01/17 at https://www.theguardian.com/commentisfree/2016/oct/31/prevent-save-lives-families-child-terrorism-programme.

Conversation (2016) *The Life Experiences That Can Prevent Sympathies for Terrorism from Developing.* London: The Conversation Trust. Accessed on 19/01/17 at http://theconversation.com/the-life-experiences-that-can-prevent-sympathies-for-terrorism-from-developing-65587.

Dalrymple, W. (2010) *Nine Lives: In Search of the Sacred in Modern India.* London: Bloomsbury.

Dart, T. (2016) '"My crime was wearing a turban": Sikh man arrested on US bus pursues justice.' *Guardian,* 30 April. Accessed on 19/01/17 at https://www.theguardian.com/us-news/2016/apr/29/sikh-man-arrested-bus-terrorist-bomb-islamophobia.

DCLG (2008) *Face to Face and Side by Side.* London: Department for Communities and Local Government. Accessed on 19/01/17 at http://webarchive.nationalarchives.gov. uk/20120919132719/http:/www.communities.gov.uk/documents/communities/pdf/898668.pdf.

DCLG (2012) *Creating the Conditions for Integration.* London: Department for Communities and Local Government. Accessed on 19/01/17 at https://www.gov.uk/government/uploads/system/uploads/attachment_data/file/7504/2092103.pdf.

Dean, S. (2016) 'British police force says it may allow female officers to wear burkas as part of uniform.' *Daily Telegraph*, 9 September. Accessed on 20/01/17 at www.telegraph.co.uk/news/2016/09/09/british-police-force-says-it-may-allow-female-officers-to-wear-f.

Defence Academy (n.d.) 'Royal College of Defence Studies.' Accessed on 19/01/17 at www.da.mod.uk/Colleges-Business-Units/RCDS.

Dhaliwal, S. (2015) 'Sikhs exhorted to observe "black" Diwali.' *Tribune India*, 11 November. Accessed on 20/01/17 at www.tribuneindia.com/news/punjab/sikhs-exhorted-to-observe-black-diwali/157172.html.

Dodd, V. (2015) 'School questioned Muslim pupil about ISIS after discussion on eco-activism.' *Guardian*, 22 September. Accessed on 31/01/17 at https://www.theguardian.com/education/2015/sep/22/school-questioned-muslim-pupil-about-isis-after-discussion-on-eco-activism.

Dreifus, C. (1993) *New York Times Interview with the Dali Lama.* Toronto: CanTibNet Newsletter. Accessed on 20/01/17 at www.sacred-texts.com/bud/tib/nytimes.htm.

Dundas, P. (2002) *The Jains.* London: Routledge.

Faith Matters (2016) *Sectarianism, Extremism and Hate Crime: The Impacts on the Ahmadiyya Community.* London: Faith Matters. Accessed on 19/01/17 at http://faith-matters.org/wp-content/uploads/2016/10/Sectarianism-Extremism-and-Hate-Crime.pdf.

Flannagan, A. (ed.) (2015) *Those Who Show Up.* Edinburgh: Muddy Pearl.

Fraser, I. (2015) 'Why is Indian prime minister Narendra Modi in London, and why are people going to see him at Wembley?' *Daily Telegraph*, 12 November. Accessed on 20/01/17 at www.telegraph.co.uk/news/worldnews/asia/india/11984475/Why-is-Indian-prime-minister-Modi-in-London-and-why-are-people-going-to-see-him-at-Wembley-stadium.html.

Freytas-Tamura, K. de (2016) 'London becomes a leading destination for French Jews after attacks.' *New York Times*, 22 April. Accessed on 20/01/17 at www.nytimes.com/2016/04/23/world/europe/london-france-jews-terrorism-anti-semitism.html?_r=1.

Frodsham, I. (2016) '15,000 people join annual Vaisakhi Sikh parade in Leicester.' *Leicester Mercury*, 24 April. Accessed on 20/01/17 at www.leicestermercury.co.uk/vaisakhi-parade-attracts-15-000-people/story-29167330-detail/story.html.

Gani, A. and Slawson, N. (2016) 'Lancashire police criticise BBC over "terrorist house" story.' *Guardian*, 21 January. Accessed on 19/01/17 at https://www.theguardian.com/uk-news/2016/jan/21/lancashire-police-criticise-bbc-over-terrorist-house-story.

Gest, J. (2010) *Apart: Alienated and Engaged Muslims in the West.* London: Hurst and Company.

Grindrod, P. and Sloggett, D. (2010) *From Grievance to Martyrdom: A Mathematical Perspective of the Journey of Radicalisation.* Reading: School of Mathematical and Physical Sciences, University of Reading. Accessed on 19/01/17 at www.reading.ac.uk/web/files/maths/preprint_10_24_grindrod.pdf.

Groves, P. (2014) 'A Search for Good Disagreement.' In Archbishop's Council (ed.) *Grace and Disagreement: Shared Conversations on Scripture, Mission and Human Sexuality. A Reader: Writings to Resource Conversations.* London: Church House Publishing.

Hall, S., King, J. and Finlay, R. (2015) *City Street Data Profile on Ethnicity, Economy and Migration: Narborough Road, Leicester.* London: London School of Economics. Accessed on 19/01/17 at https://files.lsecities.net/files/2015/12/SuperDiverseStreets_Leicester.pdf.

Halliday, J. and Dodd, V. (2015) 'UK anti-radicalisation Prevent
strategy a "toxic brand".' *Guardian*, 9 March. Accessed on
19/01/17 at https://www.theguardian.
com/uk-news/2015/
mar/09/anti-radicalisation-prevent-strategy-a-toxic-brand.

Hansard (2015) *Record of Business on 16th December 2015*, Column
2119. Accessed on 20/01/17 at www.publications.parliament.
uk/pa/ld201516/ldhansrd/text/151216-0002.htm.

HHR (2016) 'Hinduphobic contender for UK's new prime
minister championships.' Hindu Human Rights website,
3 July. Accessed on 19/01/17 at www.hinduhumanrights.
info/hinduphobic-contender-for-uks-new-prime-minister-
championships.

HM Government (2015a) *Counter-Extremism Strategy*. London:
Home Office.

HM Government (2015b) *Prevent Duty Guidance*. London: Home
Office.

HM Government (2015c) *Channel Duty Guidance*. Accessed
on 31/01/17 at https://www.gov.uk/government/uploads/
system/uploads/attachment_data/file/425189/Channel_Duty_
Guidance_April_2015.pdf.

IRIN (2014) 'CAR refugees overwhelm Cameroon.' IRIN website,
12 March. Accessed on 20/01/17 at www.irinnews.org/
report/99770/car-refugees-overwhelm-cameroon.

IRIN (2016) 'Will Myanmar's Rohingya finally become citizens
of their own country?' IRIN website, 7 July. Accessed on
20/01/17 at www.irinnews.org/analysis/2016/07/07/will-
myanmar%25E2%2580%2599s-rohingya-finally-become-
citizens-their-own-country.

Johnson, P. and MacAskill, E. (2016) 'Exclusive: "There will
be terrorist attacks in Britain," says MI5 chief.' *Guardian*, 1
November. Accessed on 19/01/17 at https://www.theguardian.
com/uk-news/2016/nov/01/andrew-parker-mi5-director-
general-there-will-be-terrorist-attacks-in-britain-exclusive.

Johnson, S. (2016) 'Muslim shopkeeper Asad Shah had
"disrespected Islam" according to man who admits his murder.'
Daily Telegraph, 7 July. Accessed on 20/01/17 at www.telegraph.
co.uk/news/2016/07/07/muslim-man-admits-murdering-
shopkeeper-asad-shah-who-wished-belo.

Katwala, S. (2014) *The Integration Consensus*. London: British
Future.

Kavanagh, J. (2011) 'Selection, availability, and opportunity: The conditional effect of poverty on terrorist group participation.' *The Journal of Conflict Resolution 55*, 1, 106–132.

Malnick, A. (2014) 'Story of the first Muslim soldier to be awarded the Victoria Cross.' *Daily Telegraph*, 31 October. Accessed on 20/01/17 at www.telegraph.co.uk/history/world-war-one/11198951/Story-of-the-first-Muslim-soldier-to-be-awarded-the-Victoria-Cross.html.

Milton, D. (2016) *Communication Breakdown: Unraveling the Islamic State's Media Efforts. Combating Terrorism Center Special Report.* West Point, NY: United States Military Academy, Combating Terrorism Center. Accessed on 20/01/17 at https://www.ctc.usma.edu/v2/wp-content/uploads/2016/10/ISMedia_Online.pdf.

Ministry of Defence (2014, 27 January) 'Freedom of information request.' Accessed on 18/01/17 at https://www.gov.uk/government/uploads/system/uploads/attachment_data/file/315082/PUBLIC_1391420325.pdf.

Ministry of Defence (2016, 1 April) 'UK armed forces biannual diversity statistics.' Accessed on 18/01/17 at https://www.gov.uk/government/uploads/system/uploads/attachment_data/file/530586/Biannual_Diversity_Statistics_1Apr16_revised.pdf.

Mohammed, J. (2015) 'Britain's counter extremism policies are criminalising Muslim thought and expression.' Public Spirit website, 27 October. Accessed on 20/01/17 at www.publicspirit.org.uk/britains-counter-extremism-policies-are-criminalising-muslim-thought-and-expression.

Morgan, P. and Lawton, C. (eds) (1996) *Ethical Issues in Six Religious Traditions.* Edinburgh: Edinburgh University Press.

NDTV (2014) '1984 riots a "dagger through India's chest" says PM Narendra Modi.' NDTV, 31 October. Accessed on 20/01/17 at www.ndtv.com/india-news/1984-riots-a-dagger-through-indias-chest-says-pm-narendra-modi-687068.

NHS (n.d.a) 'Islam.' NHS Blood and Transplant website. Accessed on 20/01/17 at https://www.organdonation.nhs.uk/about-donation/what-does-my-religion-say/islam.

NHS (n.d.b) 'Sikhism.' NHS Blood and Transplant website. Accessed on 20/01/17 at https://www.organdonation.nhs.uk/about-donation/what-does-my-religion-say/sikhism.

NPCC (2014) 'National channel referral figures.' NPCC website. Accessed on 20/01/17 at www.npcc.police.uk/ FreedomofInformation/NationalChannelReferralFigures.aspx.

NPCC (2016) 'A message from the new senior national co-ordinator for CT policing.' NPCC website, 28 October. Accessed on 20/01/17 at http://news.npcc.police.uk/releases/ from-the-new-senior-national-co-ordinator-for-ct-policing-dac-neil-basu-qpm.

O'Toole, T. (2015) 'Prevent: From "hearts and minds" to "muscular liberalism".' Public Spirit website, 12 November. Accessed on 20/01/17 at www.publicspirit.org.uk/prevent-from-hearts-and-minds-to-muscular-liberalism.

Popham, P. (2013) 'We're all in this together.' *Independent*, 27 July. Accessed on 20/01/17 at www.independent.co.uk/news/uk/ this-britain/were-all-in-this-together-how-leicester-became-a-model-of-multiculturalism-even-if-that-was-never-8732691. html.

Psephizo (2016) 'The YouGov poll on same sex marriage.' Psephizo blog, 30 January. Accessed on 20/01/17 at www.psephizo.com/ sexuality-2/the-yougov-poll-on-same-sex-marriage.

Quinn, B. (2016) 'Nursery "raised fears of radicalisation over boy's cucumber drawing".' *Guardian*, 11 March. Accessed on 19/01/17 at https://www.theguardian.com/uk-news/2016/ mar/11/nursery-radicalisation-fears-boys-cucumber-drawing-cooker-bomb.

Ramadan, T. (2010) *The Quest for Meaning: Developing a Philosophy of Pluralism.* Oxford: Oxford University Press.

Ramalingam, V. (2014) *Policy Briefing: Countering Far-Right Extremism.* London: Institute for Strategic Dialogue.

Ravat, R. (2004) *Embracing the Present, Planning the Future: Social Action by the Faith Communities of Leicester.* Leicester: Diocese of Leicester.

Richardson, L. (2006) *What Terrorists Want: Understanding the Enemy, Containing the Threat.* London: Random House.

Rumbelow, H. (2016) 'Britain's secret "school" for young extremists.' *The Times*, 25 October. Accessed on 20/01/17 at www.thetimes.co.uk/article/britains-secret-school-for-teen-extremists-5b09xbmxh.

Schools Improvement (2015) 'Everybody has A*s – employers want character.' Schools Improvement website, 28 March. Accessed on 20/01/17 at http://schoolsimprovement.net/everybody-has-as-employers-want-character.

Shah, N. (1998) *Jainism: The World of Conquerors. Volume II.* Brighton: Sussex Academic Press.

Sherwood, H. (2016a) 'Homeless shelter open with multifaith support in Leicester.' *Guardian*, 15 December. Accessed on 19/01/17 at https://www.theguardian.com/society/2016/dec/15/multifaith-homeless-shelter-leicester-churches-synagogue-muslim.

Sherwood, H. (2016b) 'Church of England members back same sex marriage.' *Guardian*, 29 January. Accessed on 19/01/17 at https://www.theguardian.com/world/2016/jan/29/church-of-england-members-back-same-sex-marriage-poll.

Sikh24 (2015) 'Sikh Council UK draws flak for meeting privately with PM Modi.' Sikh24 website, 13 November. Accessed on 20/01/17 at https://www.sikh24.com/2015/11/13/sikh-council-uk-draws-flak-for-meeting-privately-with-pm-modi/#.WEkRwuGLT-Z.

Sillitoe, D. (2015) 'Diwali celebrations: The lights and sounds of Leicester's Golden Mile.' *Guardian*, 4 November. Accessed on 19/01/17 at https://www.theguardian.com/lifeandstyle/ng-interactive/2015/nov/04/diwali-celebrations-the-lights-and-sounds-of-leicesters-golden-mile.

Squires, N. (2014) 'Pope speaks out against "horrific" abortion.' *Daily Telegraph*, 13 January. Accessed on 20/01/17 at www.telegraph.co.uk/news/worldnews/the-pope/10569196/Pope-speaks-out-against-horrific-abortion.html.

Staufenburg, J. (2016) 'Gujarat massacre.' *Independent*, 17 June. Accessed on 20/01/17 at www.independent.co.uk/news/world/asia/gujarat-massacre-india-court-jails-11-life-sentence-killings-muslims-gulbarg-society-compound-a7086876.html.

Straw, J. (2006) 'I felt uneasy talking to someone I couldn't see.' *Guardian*, 6 October. Accessed on 19/01/17 at https://www.theguardian.com/commentisfree/2006/oct/06/politics.uk.

Theos (2009) *Coming Off the Bench.* London: Theos. Accessed on 20/01/17 at www.theosthinktank.co.uk/publications/2007/02/09/coming-off-the-bench.

Theos (2015) *Who Wants a Christian Coronation?* London: Theos. Accessed on 20/01/17 at www.theosthinktank.co.uk/publications/2015/09/01/who-wants-a-christian-coronation.

USCCB (2013) *A Compilation of Quotes and Texts of Pope Francis on Dialogue, Encounter, and Interreligious and Ecumenical Relations.* Washington DC: United States Conference of Catholic Bishops. Accessed on 20/01/17 at www.usccb.org/beliefs-and-teachings/ecumenical-and-interreligious/resources/upload/Quotes-of-Pope-Francis-on-dialogue-encounter-ecumenical-and-interreligious-affairs-12042013.pdf.

Visit Leicester (2016) 'Diwali Leicester.' Accessed on 24/01/17 at www.visitleicester.info/things-to-see-and-do/festivals-celebrations/diwali.

Warzynski, P. A. (2016) 'Leicestershire Police bosses would consider including the burka in the uniform.' *Leicester Mercury*, 22 September. Accessed on 20/01/17 at www.leicestermercury.co.uk/leicestershire-police-bosses-would-consider-including-the-burka-in-the-uniform/story-29741425-detail/story.html.

Welby, J. (2015) Speech at the Board of Deputies of British Jews dinner, 6 May. Accessed on 20/01/17 at www.archbishopofcanterbury.org/articles.php/5547/archbishops-speech-at-board-of-deputies-dinner.

Wilson, T. (2015) *What Kind of Friendship? Christian Responses to Tariq Ramadan's Call for Reform within Islam.* Eugene, OR: Wipf and Stock.

Withnall, A. (2016) 'Lancashire police say "terrorist house" incident not about spelling mistake.' *Independent*, 21 January. Accessed on 20/01/17 at www.independent.co.uk/news/uk/home-news/lancashire-police-say-terrorist-house-incident-not-about-spelling-mistake-a6824481.html.

Woolcock, N. (2014) 'Teach team spirit, character and the meaning of work, business urges.' *The Times*, 8 August. Accessed on 20/01/17 at www.thetimes.co.uk/tto/education/article4171485.ece.

SUBJECT INDEX

abortion
  Buddhist views of 67
  Christian views of 68–9
  general views of 76
  Hindu views of 70
  Islamic views of 71
  Jain views of 72–3
  Jewish views of 74
  Sikh views of 75
agreement
  term rejected by St Philip's
    Centre 36–7
Ahmed, Tanver 128
Anglicanism
  conference on living well
    together 39–44
  good disagreement within 82–3
  and human sexuality 155
  role in society 155–6
  and sanctity of life 68–9
  understanding difference within
    82–3
armed forces
  and encountering difference
    58–63
  faith communities in 59–60
  training on faith communities
    46–7
Atkinson, Richard 20

Baha'is
  in Leicester 23
Basu, Neil 120
Board of Deputies of British Jews
  30
British National Party 19
Buddhism
  and sanctity of life 66–8
  understanding difference within
    94–6
Butler, Tom 20

Cameron, David 59, 146
Casey Review 11
Catalyst programme 140–3
Chaplin, Shirley 101
child sexual exploitation 126–7
Christian Engagement in a Multi-
  Faith World 49–53
Christian-Muslim Forum 30
Christianity
  in armed forces 59, 60, 61
  and encountering difference 32
  in Leicester 20–1
  and sanctity of life 68–9
  tensions within 153
  understanding difference within
    86–8 see also Anglicanism
    and Roman Catholicism
Church of England see
  Anglicanism

Church Urban Fund 30, 129
Cole, Simon 113
community cohesion
and 'Leicester model' 24–6
contraception
Buddhist views of 67–8
general views of 76–7
Islamic views of 71–2
Roman Catholic views of 64–5,
68–9
Crabb, Stephen 153
Cridland, John 141
cultural differences
and encountering difference
50–3

Daily Telegraph 79
Diwali festival 22

Embracing the Present, Planning the
Future (Ravat) 146
encountering difference
and armed forces 58–63
and Christian Engagement in a
Multi-Faith World 49–53
and cultural difference 50–3
developing into understanding
and trust 37–8
facilitating 54–8
in St Philip's Centre 31–2
within faith communities 38, 53
Etheridge, Sally 132–3
euthanasia
Buddhist views of 67
Christian views of 69
general views of 76
Hindu views of 70
Islamic views of 72
Jain views of 73
Jewish views of 74–5
Sikh views of 76
Eweida, Nadia 101
extremism
and Prevent strategy 113–19

facilitating encountering difference
54–8
'Facts of Faith' game 45, 60
faith communities
in armed forces 59–60
encountering difference within
38, 53
in Leicester 20–4
public sector training on 44–8
Federation of Muslim
Organisations (FMO) 21
Festival of Season's Greetings 132
Francis, Pope 146–7
future imagining 154–8

good disagreement
in Anglicanism 82–3
Guardian, The 80, 113

Hall, John 21
Harris, Herbert 84
Hart, Sir Israel 84
hate crimes
and interfaith co-operation
127–9
statistics on 153–4
Henig, Sir Mark 84
Himmah 37
Hinduism
in armed forces 50–60, 62
encountering difference within
38, 53
and interfaith co-operation
126–7
in Leicester 22
and sanctity of life 69–71
tensions within 152
understanding difference within
92–4
and visit of Narenda Modi
79–82
and work uniforms 100–1
Howe, Earl 47, 58

Independent (newspaper) 17
Inter Faith Network for the UK 30
interfaith co-operation
    and Catalyst programme 140–3
    and child sexual exploitation
        126–7
    and Festival of Season's
        Greetings 132
    and hate crimes 17–9
    and Mammas project 132–6
    and Near Neighbours
        programme 37, 129–38
    and One Roof Leicester 136–8
    resources for 150–1
    at St. Philip's Centre 125, 126–9,
        140–5
    and Salaam Shalom Kitchen
        initiative 37, 131–2
    tensions within 152–4
    and victimhood 151–2
Islam
    in armed forces 59, 60, 63
    and encountering difference 37
    and interfaith co-operation
        126–9
    in Leicester 21–2
    and Prevent strategy 109–22
    and sanctity of life 71–2
    tensions within 152–3
    understanding difference within
        89–92
    and visit of Narenda Modi 80,
        81–2
    and work uniforms 100, 101–2

Jainism
    in Leicester 23
    and sanctity of life 72–3
    understanding difference within
        98–9
Judaism
    in armed forces 59, 60, 61–2
    dietary laws 33–6
    and encountering difference
        33–6, 37, 53
    in Leicester 23, 84

and sanctity of life 74–5
understanding difference within
    84, 85–6

Lawrence, Stephen 47
'learning to live well together'
    Church of England conference
        on 39–44
    complexity of 16
    and religious faith 40–1
    in school 41–4
    as value of St Philip's Centre
        30–3
Leicester
    Asian population in 18–19, 24,
        25–6
    diversity of 17
    early history of 17
    faith communities in 20–4, 84
    'Leicester model' 24–6
    migration into 17–20
    public sector training in 44–8
'Leicester model' of community
    cohesion 24–6
Loughborough 24

Mammas project 132–6
May, Theresa 48
McCallum, John 137
medical ethics 63–77
Modi, Narenda 79–82
Morrison, Kathy 20
Muslims *see* Islam

Naik, Rahoul 143
Nash, Lord 39–40
National Front 19
Navratri festival 22
Near Neighbours programme 30
    description of 129–31
    and Festival of Season's
        Greetings 132
    and One Roof Leicester 136–8
    and Salaam Shalom Kitchen
        initiative 37, 131–2

One Roof Leicester 136–8
organ donation
    Buddhist views of 68
    general views of 77
    Hindu views of 70–1
    Islamic views of 72
    Jain views of 73
    Sikh views of 76

Paganism
    in Leicester 23
    understanding difference within
        98
police force
    training on faith communities
Prevent strategy
    concerns about 111–15
    engagement with 119–22
    and extremism threat 113–19
    and St. Philip's Centre 109–11,
        121–2
public sector
    training on faith communities
        44–8

Ravat, Salma 136–8
respect
    limitations of 106
    term rejected by St Philip's
        Centre 36
Richerby, Glynn 137
Roman Catholicism
    and abortion 68
    and contraception 64–5, 68

St Philip's Centre
    aims of 11–12, 27–8
    Catalyst programme 140–3
    encountering difference in 31–2
    founded 20–1, 27
    future imagining 154–8
    interfaith co-operation at 125,
        126–9, 140–5

'learning to live well together'
    30–3
and Prevent strategy 109–11,
    121–2
public sector training 44–8
social action days in 144–7
stakeholders in 29–30
theological foundations of 28–9
trust-building in 36–7, 106–8
understanding difference in
    32–6, 99–100
values of 30–8
Salaam Shalom Kitchen (SaSh) 37,
    131–2
sanctity of life
    Buddhist views of 66–8
    Christian views of 64–5, 68–9
    definition of 66
    general views of 76–7
    Hindu views of 69–71
    Islamic views of 71–2
    Jain views of 72–3
    Jewish views of 74–5
    Sikh views of 75–6
Saturday Stop By Project 137
schools
    and Catalyst programme 140–3
    learning to live well together in
        41–4
Shah, Asad 128, 154
Sikhism
    in armed forces 60, 52
    and interfaith co-operation
        126–7
    in Leicester 22–3
    and medical ethics 64
    and sanctity of life 75–6
    understanding difference within
        96–8
    and visit of Narenda Modi 80–2
    and work uniforms 100–1
Snow, Martyn 20
social action days
    in St Philip's Centre 144–7
Stevens, Tim 20
Straw, Jack 101

Thompson, David 101
Those Who Show Up (Flannagan)
        152
Times, The 121
tolerance
    limitations of 104–5
    strengths of 105–6
    term rejected by St Philip's
            Centre 36
trust-building
    establishing 108–9, 122–4
    and Prevent strategy 109–22
    in St Philip's Centre 36–7, 106–8
    and tolerance 104–5

Uddin, Sharmina 143
understanding difference
    in Anglicanism 82–3
    in Buddhism 94–6
    in Christianity 86–8

in Hinduism 92–4
in Islam 89–92
in Jainism 98–9
in Judaism 84, 85–6
motivation for 37–8
in Paganism 98
in St Philip's Centre 32–6,
        99–100
in Sikhism 96–8
and visit of Narenda Modi
        79–82
and work uniforms 100–2

Vaisakhi festival 23
victimhood 151–2

Wilson, Tom 21
Wingate, Andrew 20
work uniforms 100–2

AUTHOR INDEX

Anglo-Sikh Wars 23
Associated Press in Jerusalem 85

Baldet, W. 115
Bard, M.G. 33
BBC 24, 48, 65, 67, 68, 70, 72, 74,
    75, 76, 110, 111, 127
Berger, J.M. 116, 119
Bhul, K. 119
Bretherton, L. 104, 105
British Social Attitudes (BSA) 156

Cantle, T. 12, 140
Casey, L. 11, 102, 112
Census 59
Chakrabortty, N. 80
Chakroborti, A. 154
Chauhan, S. 81
Cole, S. 113
Conversation 119

Dalrymple, W. 73
Dart, T. 153
Dean, S. 102
Department for Communities and
    Local Government (DCLG)
    140, 143
Dhaliwal, S. 81
Dodd, V. 110, 112

Dreifus, C. 67
Dundas, P. 73

Faith Matters 128
Finlay, R. 17
Flannagan, A. 152
Fraser, I. 79
Freytas-Tamura, K. de 86
Frodhsam, I. 23

Gani, A. 112
Garland, J. 154
Gest, J. 118
Grindrod, P. 119
Groves, P. 82

Hall, S. 17
Halliday, J. 110
Hansard 40
Hardy, S.-J. 154
Hindu Human Rights (HHR) 153
HM Government 110, 111, 116,
    120

IRIN 114

Johnson, P. 114
Johnson, S. 128

Katwala, S. 139
Kavanagh, J. 118
King, J. 17

Lawton, C. 75

MacAskill, E. 114
Malnick, A. 47
Milton, D. 116, 117
Ministry of Defence 59
Mohammed, J. 110
Morgan, P. 75

National Police Chiefs' Council
      120
NDTV 80
NHS 72, 76

O'Toole, T. 110

Psephizo 155

Quinn, B. 112

Ramadan, T. 104, 105
Ramalingam, V. 117

Ravat, R. 140, 146
Richardson, L. 118
Rumbelow, H. 121

Schools Improvement 141
Shah, N. 73
Sherwood, H. 138, 155
Sikh24 81
Sillitoe, D. 22
Slawson, N. 112
Sloggett, D. 119
Squires, N. 68
Stauenburg, J. 114
Straw, J. 101

Theos 155, 156

United States Conference of
      Catholic Bishops (USCCB)
      147

Visit Leicester 22

Warzynski, P.A. 102
Welby, J. 149
Wilson, T. 106
Withnall, A. 112
Woolcock, N. 141

CPI Antony Rowe
Eastbourne, UK
January 05, 2024